'I couldn't put this book down and Yes, this is a memoir of childhood memoir of loneliness, of confusion and grief. Of emotions that ricochet through us all, at one time or another. With powerful, raw and incisive writing, Gemma is unflinching in her personal investigation of family and trauma. She peels back layer upon layer to ask: *What happens to our souls when we feel we don't matter? How do we break the silence and put our broken selves back together?* This is a brave and addictive book which speaks of one life, and all lives at the same time. It also asks uncomfortable but crucial questions about children, sex and consent and a society that often chooses to look the other way.'

Ginger Gorman, journalist and author of *Troll Hunting*

'*No Matter Our Wreckage* is personal and political, unflinching and generous. Carey writes with a researcher's curiosity and a survivor's urgency about intergenerational trauma and the persistent, insistent, silence around sexual abuse.'

Emily Maguire, author of *An Isolated Incident*

'*No Matter Our Wreckage* is a brutal reminder of our responsibility to notice and protect those we love. A devastating and clear-eyed memoir with a poet's heart. Gemma Carey will boil your blood and break your heart.'

Anna Spargo-Ryan, author of *Troll Hunting*

NO MATTER OUR WRECKAGE

NO MATTER OUR WRECKAGE

A MEMOIR ABOUT GROOMING, BETRAYAL, TRAUMA AND LOVE

GEMMA CAREY

ALLEN&UNWIN
SYDNEY·MELBOURNE·AUCKLAND·LONDON

First published in 2020

Copyright © Gemma Carey 2020

All rights reserved. No part of this book may be reproduced or transmitted in any form or by any means, electronic or mechanical, including photocopying, recording or by any information storage and retrieval system, without prior permission in writing from the publisher. The Australian *Copyright Act 1968* (the Act) allows a maximum of one chapter or 10 per cent of this book, whichever is the greater, to be photocopied by any educational institution for its educational purposes provided that the educational institution (or body that administers it) has given a remuneration notice to the Copyright Agency (Australia) under the Act.

Allen & Unwin
83 Alexander Street
Crows Nest NSW 2065
Australia
Phone: (61 2) 8425 0100
Email: info@allenandunwin.com
Web: www.allenandunwin.com

 A catalogue record for this book is available from the National Library of Australia

ISBN 978 1 76087 767 5

Set in 12/18.5 pt Sabon by Midland Typesetters, Australia
Printed and bound in Australia by Griffin Press, part of Ovato

10 9 8 7 6 5 4 3 2 1

 The paper in this book is FSC® certified. FSC® promotes environmentally responsible, socially beneficial and economically viable management of the world's forests.

PART ONE

Me

CHAPTER ONE

This woman's pain could kill you

There is an image of my mother that will haunt me for the rest of my life.

She's standing in the kitchen of my parents' big rambling family home, clinging to the wall, crying. She's hanging on to that kitchen wall with all the strength she has – an egg-sized tumour in her brain has taken away her balance. Without the wall to steady herself, she'll collapse. If she tries to follow me, as I stride past her, she'll fall and hurt herself.

We both know it. We both know that she is trapped there, in the kitchen, hanging on to the wall. And that if I leave, she might be stuck there for hours.

That morning her short grey hair is uncharacteristically unkempt. Her face is puffy. She looks terrified. It's an awful, pitiful sight. This normally dignified woman in her early sixties, begging her daughter through sobs not to go.

I can't bear to witness it. I avoid looking at her, determined to make it out the front door without giving in to her pleading. If I stay, there are only two options: allow her to sweep everything under the rug again or lose my composure and spill twenty years' worth of hurt right there on that kitchen floor. I don't want to do either. I just want to get away.

We've been doing battle all night. Though over what exactly, neither of us could tell you. The drugs they have given her to shrink the brain tumour strip her down to base emotion. To fear, rage and sadness. Last night it was rage. This morning it is fear.

She is begging me to at least turn and face her. To say goodbye before I leave. That's always been her rule – never leave the house in anger without saying goodbye, lest something terrible happens and you are left regretting the fact you parted on bad terms.

Ignoring her, I collect my keys and bag.

As I reach the front door, I hear her call out after me, 'You need to be a more forgiving daughter.'

I don't answer. I don't look back.

I pull the front door shut behind me as I walk out, stumbling into the warm sun of a Monday morning. I get in my car and drive to work, bleeding exhaustion and sadness.

I didn't stop or look back when my mother called out to me because she wasn't asking me to forgive her for the rage and psychosis of the night before. Or at least, she wasn't asking me to forgive her *only* for the night before. Between the tears on her face and the cold of my back were twenty years' worth of secrets and betrayal.

You see, when I was twelve a man twice my age used to sneak into my bedroom several times a week and go down on me. My mother knew, but she never spoke to me about it. And she never intervened to stop the abuse.

Now she is dying, and the past is rising to the surface like a bruise.

Fragments of memory swirl and bubble up. Out of order, unstoppable.

A girl in purple Doc Martens boots standing by the road in the middle of the night.

A knock on the window, a waft of men's cologne.

My mother looking at me anxiously, a question on her lips she doesn't ask.

A series of wordless snapshots I am trying to make sense of.

It has taken me years to begin to find the right words to describe the events that interrupted my experience of 'child', 'adolescent' and, in time, 'relationship'. Some of the words weren't invented when I was twelve and this story began. 'Grooming' has become part of our modern lexicon as knowledge of the internet – and the dangers it contains – has grown, but it didn't exist then.

The first time I read about grooming I sat in silence as a thousand pieces of an impossibly complex jigsaw shuffled around in my head to find their rightful place. At that time, I was living in Brunswick, Melbourne, where I moved in my early twenties to escape the suffocation of my home town. I was working from home, studying for my PhD, and clicking around the internet for a distraction. Falling down the clickbait rabbit hole, I ended up on the website of an artist who was collecting photos of women holding signs. The signs had words their abusers had said to them, had used to coax them, lure them in.

I could have held nearly every one of those signs myself.

Buried in the text describing the artist's intent was a description of grooming. I leant back in my chair. I stared at the ceiling whispering over and over: 'This is a *thing*.'

There is great power in giving something a name. It brings a sense of order. When we don't have a name for things, we often blame ourselves. But once named, analysis and judgement follow.

We know about grooming over the internet now – it's a crime. Grooming is an evil act that leads to other, greater, evil acts. But, when I was growing up in the 1990s and the early 2000s, we didn't yet have the word grooming.

Other words, those needed to form sentences, paragraphs – understanding, as it were – were beyond my reach. They only started to come when I was thirty-two, and my mother began dying from cancer.

Finding these words is much harder, particularly against the societal backdrop of female exploitation, male excuses and the degradation of women. In a world where the concept of women's consent is still treated as hazy and pliable – not a simple statement of fact, of 'yes' or 'no'. This haziness has played out in numerous court cases and opinion pieces in recent years, with men let off the hook due to alcohol – sometimes their own drunkenness, but usually the woman's – or a 'misunderstanding', leaving women unheard and no doubt confused.

We know that most cases of sexual assault are never reported, or if they are women are discouraged from proceeding with charges because they won't 'stick'. Meanwhile, in so-called advanced democracies like the United States, rape kits have sat unanalysed for decades. It's not a one-off tragedy like some reporting would have you believe, it's a daily occurrence. Though, gradually, this is shifting.

As more women – powerful women – come forward, baring their secrets and their stories. Finally, it appears, the world is starting to listen.

Yet for me, the words I needed weren't just to describe an act. Grooming, molesting, sexual assault, statutory rape. Useful? Yes. Sufficient? No. These words describe a series of acts; they do not tell us *why* those acts were committed. Importantly, they didn't help me to make sense of why these acts had happened to me, specifically.

The words I needed had to come from a deep understanding of why these things happened to me. For years I believed my perpetrator had betrayed me, which is to suggest that I held certain expectations of him as a fellow human being; as though he was a friend who had overstepped, rather than a predator who accomplished his goals. I needed to understand that the betrayal did not come from the man who molested me. No, the betrayal came from the woman who could have protected me.

———

The words I needed began to form after a friend said, 'But your mother did this.'

Sarah and I were hanging out at her house. She lived down the road from me in Brunswick and we were both studying in the same postgraduate program. She once joked, when explaining to a stranger how we knew each other, 'We started talking one day and never stopped.' Several times a week we would stroll over to one another's house, sip tea and talk. Back then, Sarah was warm and almost too friendly, wearing all her anxieties on her sleeve. Charismatic, with a glint of *I am not okay* behind the eyes – just like me.

On this particular occasion I had come to her house. I walked straight in, curled up on her large grey sofa, and waited for a giant cup of hot tea to be passed to me and the discussion of our dysfunctional families to begin. Such was our ritual. Sarah and I spent a great deal of time talking about our families and our mothers. We were both from middle-class homes with complex family relations, masked our insecurities with over-achievement. She was one of the few people in my life at that time who knew I had been abused – and perhaps the only person who understood the complicated dynamics between my mother and me, because they mirrored her own experiences. That day, like many before, we were reflecting on our families. This sometimes had a way of winding back to my childhood abuse.

I sat tucked up on the sofa as Sarah strolled around the downstairs living room of her duplex apartment – freshly renovated and smelling of paint and sanded timber. She looked back over her shoulder as she placed something in an overhead kitchen cupboard, that statement about my mother's culpability called across the room like it was the most obvious thing in the world.

She went on, turning to face me, 'I wanted someone to come save me too – that's what my family did to me, I felt so alone. But my mother made me too frightened of everyone and everything.'

I continued to sit on that couch, silently pondering which was the more serious crime a parent could commit: to have made a child feel alone and frightened, like Sarah – too afraid to venture out into the world and therefore into the path of danger? Or to have made her feel so alone, like me, that she sought out something different, something better than 'family', and found harm instead?

Reading about grooming, and the five words Sarah gave me that day, released me from a lifetime of self-blame, of shitty boyfriends and society telling me I was – at least in part – responsible for what had happened to me. I'd been volatile. I'd taken risks. I bore the consequences of my choices, because that's what happens to bad young girls.

Back in the 1990s and early 2000s, before third wave feminism, broad public disclosure of sexual assault and a growing understanding that these things in fact happen to any woman – to all women – this was the dominant narrative.

I'm reminded of the iconic, formative social and cultural moments of that time. Monica Lewinsky, just a twenty-two-year-old White House intern in 1995, publicly condemned when a powerful man wielded that power for sexual pleasure. I remember my mother and her friends at the time being disgusted with Clinton, but that disgust came with a distaste for Lewinsky too – what kind of young woman would take part in something so stupid and sordid? Would *let* that happen?

In 2017, more than twenty years later, Lewinsky finally felt she could return to the spotlight to speak about her experiences and the public shaming of women. When she was finally given back her voice, she told us that she had felt she needed to protect the president. Protect him from his own indiscretions. From his own actions.

Before that, in 1993, we were all glued to our televisions watching David Lynch's extraordinary TV series *Twin Peaks*, a cultural touchstone, in which teenager Laura Palmer – the central character – is defined primarily by her promiscuity, which is implicitly positioned as leading to her death at the hands of a man.

The message of that time was clear: women are responsible for the things that men do, and never more so than if they express sexual desire.

Then there are other, equally iconic, cultural artefacts that continue to have social resonance. I think about *Lolita* sometimes. I wonder about how much damage is done by interpretations like this of the 'older man, seductive young girl' cliché. Not just to whether people can hear – really hear – the stories of young women but also to the way women narrate and understand their own stories of abuse.

Since 2016 we have had women's marches across the western world in response to the election of an American president widely and unashamedly known to have committed countless acts of abuse against women, and then the appointment of a Supreme Court judge accused of rape.

We have seen campaigns against sexual assault in which everyone from celebrities to schoolteachers have publicly declared 'Me Too'. A few have gone so far as to name powerful men and reveal their actions – their crimes. Unsurprising to many women, the chorus of 'Me Too' has been deafening.

At its peak I couldn't help but question the women in my life who *didn't* declare that they had been victims of some form of abuse by men – or, more alarmingly, those who felt that what they had experienced didn't qualify as abuse, wasn't a serious enough offence. But when I scratched the surface, just lightly, I found that the facade crumbled. To some degree we have all been victims. Some of us simply bear more scars.

While I wish 'Me Too' had existed when I was younger, so I could see my story reflected in those of others, the movement has made some women conflicted at times. Yet again women are being asked to carry the burden of social change – to convince men and the broader systems in which we live that women's voices and experiences matter, that men's actions towards women matter. Irrespective of the tensions, these recent campaigns have been watershed moments. I have to believe that they hold the power to effect cultural change. If not full-scale revolution, may they at least have the power to reshape the way women make sense of their own abuse.

———

For many years, I continued to believe I was responsible for what had happened to me. Until public discussions began to shift, until Sarah, my closest female friend, said those new words to me: 'But your mother did this.' I will love Sarah for the rest of my life for giving me those five words. Those were the words I needed to begin to understand what had happened to me.

I used to think that the person, the perpetrator, could tell me why this had happened. When I was young, and again twenty years after it all began – when my mother was dying, creating a space for me to finally seek out deeper truths – I would ask him, '*Why?*' Why this act, why this girl? Please, tell me why this happened to me.

And here I am, in my thirties, finally with the words to explain why. Or at the very least, the realisation that I'd been asking the wrong person. His 'why?' He was a child abuser, and I was a child who became available to him to abuse. It's as simple and as complicated as that, though I know his own childhood was complex and dark, perhaps setting him on a certain path. Twenty years later I understand this predator–prey dynamic. I don't feel the need to ask him why those acts.

But that still leaves *Why this girl?*

The answer to this question is rarely explored.

We hear simple timelines of events: where the woman was when it happened; what she was doing beforehand; what she was wearing; whether she was drunk. In essence, we hear the role she may have played in her own abuse.

In cases where the victim is a minor we hear predominately about the man. His history, his actions, how he pursued his quarry.

Both these narratives fall short. We need to delve more deeply, search out more complex truths.

―

I remember, when I was nineteen or so, living in Adelaide with my sister. Our parents had moved to Canberra for work, leaving us the family home. For the first time I began to test out what it would feel like, what would happen, if I told people my secret. At first, I tried to hint at why I wasn't quite 'normal' to guys who were interested in me – almost like a warning. At the time I believed that to understand me you had to know this essential inner core of my experience; this thing that seemed to define me and have nothing to do with me all at once.

Next, I tried to give these hints a more solid shape.

Walking from our house in the Adelaide Hills to the bus stop to head into town for a night out, I finally tried out a full confession on a girlfriend. She'd just told me she suffered from severe OCD and had started taking medication – but she was telling me and no one else because 'people wouldn't understand'. Thinking she was, like me, 'not quite normal', I tried to reciprocate.

'So what?' she replied when I told her, before moving the conversation back to her struggle to write a sentence for her uni assignment without erasing it three times first. Her easy dismissal might have been a reflection on my telling, but now I suspect it said more about how such experiences were viewed back then, and perhaps still are viewed by some.

Around the same time, at a house party my sister and I threw, I tried again. I was hanging out on the deck that stretched around the second storey of our family home with our mutual friend Pete. Leaning on the wooden rail, looking out over the blackness of unlit bushland, we swapped little secrets. Jeff Buckley was filtering out into the warm night air, the mood having reached the melancholic tones that all house parties seem to descend into after 2 am. He declared proudly that he'd given a blow job to a famous football player in a trashy Adelaide nightclub. Drawing a deep breath, I blurted out at high speed 'When-I-was-twelve-a-man-twice-my-age-used-to-sneak-over-here-and-go-down-on-me.'

'Wow, I'm jealous,' an appreciative tone to his voice.

Feeling silly, I turned and walked back inside the house, greeted by a huddle of drunken uni students crooning, *Hallelujah . . . Hallelujah, Hallelujah.*

In the days that followed the party, Pete promptly spread the word around other friends. Like casual gossip instead of a deeply held, nearly unspeakable secret.

Now I see the layering of smaller betrayals on top of larger ones. At the time, I was still too confused about how to understand what had happened to me to be angry. My friends' casual treatment made me wonder if it was all a casual matter.

———

Later, I tried something different. I began to say I was forced. Sitting in a driveway in the suburbs, leading up to the house of a boy who was a friend but wanted to be more, I interrupted him as he went to kiss me: 'Someone used to force me to do things.' 'Forced' played the role of pleading – *Look, something terrible has happened here, can't you see this is a tragedy?* But I wasn't forced, at least not in the crude meaning of the word, or the base images it conjures.

Because here lies the complexity of these stories rarely told: in time, I wanted him to sneak into my bedroom. I wanted to experience the orgasms, the kissing, the touching. In time, I sought it out, I enjoyed it.

This is what is so hard to hold in one story – the dual presence of fear and pleasure. And to convey the understanding that you have control over neither.

Sitting in my psychologist's office, twenty years after the abuse, I finally began to understand more deeply what had happened to me. To find words beyond 'someone used to do things to me' or 'I was forced'. I began to develop a more sophisticated understanding.

My psychologist helped me to see that while on the surface I had a privileged middle-class upbringing, this does not mean that everything was fine. That everything was safe.

What you can see from the surface, from the outside, of my upbringing and family makes it very hard to explain the ways in which my childhood was fundamentally wrong. My parents didn't drink or do drugs, they didn't beat me. They were academics and authors.

As my psychologist said one afternoon in her secluded office, 'If you'd been beaten all your life, you'd know you'd been beaten.' But when the abuse takes a far subtler form it's insidious – deniable, hidden, dismissible. Rationalised. The words to describe this betrayal, this abuse, still aren't easy to find. I was abandoned within 'family'.

There's no common language for this as there is for 'grooming'. It's very hard to explain how you can be 'family', nested in a middle-class life with the opportunities and privileges it affords, but be alone. And yet, I doubt my story is uncommon.

Sometimes in that small office, me once again curled up on a couch, my psychologist reminds me – fiercely but with great compassion, and it's a rare kind of woman who can manage both at once – 'You didn't matter. You literally nearly had no matter.' She means this in the scientific sense: particles condensing and adhering to one another until we have substance, until we have mass that cannot be ignored.

In our house, it was my mother who mattered. She had so much matter that her presence, her emotions, tilted the very ground you stood on, creating a precarious slide into her world.

My mother has always filled a room. A short, plump woman with an endless capacity to talk, she has a sort of unstoppable verbal velocity. 'Maximum words, minimum conversation,' someone once said about her.

Sometimes, she seems infinitely capable. Running the finances for the household, along with her father's business before he died, for example. One afternoon she decided to re-cover an entire lounge set herself, and within a week it was done. When I was a toddler she and her friend declared that Adelaide needed a guidebook. So they wrote it. Then self-published it, to great acclaim. I still see it on the shelves of houses in Adelaide when I visit there.

Though this energy for life is tempered by chronic pain. When my mother was thirteen she had Ross River fever – a type of mosquito-borne virus. While no one has ever determined for certain whether this was the cause of her ailments, from her late teens onwards she experienced intermittent pain and inflammation in her joints that grew worse as she aged. There were times in my childhood when her hands would be too painful to open the car door, only for it to pass and her left foot to become suddenly too swollen to walk on. She has hidden these ever-changing pains and malfunctioning body parts from as many people as she can – as is her way. One must, always, carry on. If you pay too much attention to something, you might make it real.

My mother draws people in, particularly younger people looking for a maternal figure. She would be the 'second mum' for many of our friends at different points in our lives, cooking up hot meals, asking endless questions, giving advice – solicited or not. 'I feel like she loves me, but she's critical of me and thinks that I am silly,' said a lifelong friend of mine, 'possibly because I'm not as smart as your family.' She absolutely does love this friend – like a third daughter, in fact. But that just makes her more critical.

She projects confidence: stylish clothes, short spiky haircuts, large jewellery – she likes to make a statement. A statement matched by her sharp but critical intellect. Beneath this facade, she is bothered by her weight, anxious about whether she is intellectual or cultured enough for the people she is mixing with. This tends to come out as a strange mixture of flattery and condescension. She is known to have a special knack for homing in on someone's deepest insecurity and sinking the knife in with an offhand quip. It might be subconscious; a tic she can't control or maybe doesn't even know she has. This has made her a divisive figure. You either love her for being 'so full of life, so generous!', as her acupuncturist proclaimed to me the day I went for an appointment. Or you can't stand her because she is judgemental and rude to you. Each of these assessments is true for those on the outside. Living inside our family was different again.

Growing up on the inside, the world was devoid of anything but her insecurities and her thinly veiled self-loathing, and your task was to help lay sandbags against the reality seeping in. If you failed to stem the tide – or, worse, offered up reality with both hands, as I did – you were violently ejected. But the ground still tilted towards her, and so round and round we would go.

I was loved, but I wasn't loved correctly. I was loved as an extension of the people who created me. I wasn't loved as though I had matter, or that my matter *mattered* as much as my mother's, as it were.

Our role was to reflect well on our mother. Deeply competitive, we existed to outdo others, to compensate for her anxieties about her own self-perceived intellectual deficiencies. My sister did this beautifully – she was an exceptionally gifted child in art, music, language, you name it. I was dyslexic, with both language and numbers. The daughter of an author who couldn't spell, the daughter of a mathematician who couldn't learn her times tables. My sister would have been a hard act to follow in my parents' eyes for any child, but it was especially hard for me.

———

Back in Adelaide, in fourth grade, one of our year-long assignments was to keep a journal that our teacher would read over each week. In my journal, I talked about struggling to settle into the new, bigger school I'd just moved to. I poured my little eight-year-old self into that journal.

One entry had the teacher call my parents.

I had written that I wasn't as sad that week as I was other weeks. A minor triumph in my eyes; I was a sad child who was a little less sad that week.

At home that night after the call, my mother walked into the living room and accosted me for writing about being sad. She didn't ask her eight-year-old daughter *why* she was sad. She didn't take me to speak to anyone about *being* so sad I wrote about it in school assignments. She was angry.

After that, I got locked out of the house numerous times for getting into fights with her, for yelling at her – and with her. Our house was nestled in the bush. This wasn't being locked out in the confines of a suburban backyard – our 'backyard' was endless hills and gullies.

When I fought with her, I was using the only tools I had to be heard; if writing didn't work, then maybe meeting anger with anger would.

I've only recently discovered that children under ten aren't usually locked out of their home as punishment. That mothers should be able to cope with the reality of their eight-year-olds' lives – hold them, support them, enter their world and help them make sense of it. Not lock them out. Alone.

―

My loneliness made me excellent prey – I needed to find a place where I mattered. As a result I craved attention, which usually ended up being the wrong kind. You take what's on offer, and in our society what's most commonly on offer to girls is male sexual attention. As young women we are trained to search for self-worth in the male gaze. That term – 'male gaze' – has become common now, but back in the 1990s it wasn't thrown about the way it is now, talked about on television or discussed in think pieces. Again, we needed a label to reclaim the experience. 'Male gaze' actually arose from film scholarship to give voice to the sexual politics that shape women's lives. It is meant to capture the ways in which from the earliest of ages women's sexuality is defined and deftly crafted by men, serving to empower men but ultimately objectify women.

We might have given it a word, we might be reclaiming experiences, but sexual politics are insidious. This has never struck me more than when an impossibly brilliant, highly educated female friend of mine, with a job so influential in international politics I can't name it without identifying her, posted on Facebook in response to the 'Me Too' campaign: 'This is what patriarchy does. I have watched so many women declare their experiences of sexual assault. I have none, and I find myself thinking, "I mustn't be as attractive."'

Even at twelve, I attracted the gaze of older men. Early puberty helps with this. And in this gaze, I finally mattered. I was not an inconvenience, or a disappointment. I was more than the difficult, dyslexic child of academics.

Desired and *valued* are easily conflated if you're young and alone. They would continue to be conflated for me for many years to come. My abuse started a pattern: the confusing of 'mattering' with male desire. Over the years I have danced in the light of so many men's desires near and far, thinking that it meant I mattered. But I didn't matter, and from where I stand now, neither do any of those men.

———

'But your mother did this.'

This conflation – desired and valued – persisted even though I knew my mother had betrayed me through an act of omission. As I've said, my mother knew. Not immediately, but later – when I was still a child. She knew because my abuser wrote me letters, which she intercepted. Those letters told the whole story. They left no room for doubt. Layering secrets on secrets, she kept them hidden in her nightstand.

Frozen, she kept the intimate details of her child's trauma at the hands of an adult man to herself. After school one afternoon I found them by accident, stacked on top of loose change, broken bits of jewellery and the tiny watch batteries which had brought me to her bedroom. I took the letters back. Burnt them at the bottom of the garden; burying the secrets deeper still.

So yes, my mother did this to me. Keeping page after page of sordid details about what this perpetrator had done – what he still wanted to do. She never spoke of them. Not to me, not to my father. Not to a single soul who could have stepped in and protected me from escalating abuse.

But Sarah's words made me realise my mother – or my family, if we are to lay the blame more evenly – also committed a crime of commission.

Your parents did this.

Your parents, your mother, left you alone in the middle of what they called 'family', to be found by someone – something – else. Finally, I began to find the answer to: *Why this girl?*

With time I've come to understand more about how you can be abandoned within 'family'. I've also continued to question why my mother kept my secrets right there where she lay her head each night.

When I was young, it seemed perfectly acceptable to me that parents and children have secrets they do not share, or things that are known but never spoken of. That's how family worked, I thought. As I have got older, and thought about how I would raise my own children, I have found this bewildering. I have wondered what it is about her, or perhaps her past, that led her to do this: How does a mother keep the trauma of her child quite literally so close to her head and her heart but never speak a word of it?

―――

In Lidia Yuknavitch's memoir *The Chronology of Water* there is a line about her own mother that grabbed me perhaps more than any other sentence ever has. Yuknavitch's writing can simultaneously alienate you, because of the sheer brutality of the events that have shaped her life, and, thanks to her unflinching honesty, bring you closer to the truth of your own life than you've ever dared go.

I wrote that one sentence down. I photographed it and sent the photograph to friends who I thought needed that sentence as much as I did. I kept it close to me, reciting it to myself. A simple sentence that sums up so much of what I could never give words to:

'This woman's pain could kill you.'

CHAPTER TWO

Fragments

I don't know who David is. I know what he did. I know it has taken me twenty years to get to a point where I think I can make sense of him and what happened between us and what it has to do with 'family'.

This is what I know about him:

He might have finished school.
He didn't formally attend university, but he sat in the back of classes.
He was born in Ireland.
He spoke of his mother, but never his father.
He was thrown out of home by his mother in his teens.
He thought he was clever.
He is an only child.
He's a manic-depressive.

He has scars on his wrists.

He suffered sexual, physical and psychological abuse as a child.

He is very paranoid.

His mental illness has worsened as he has aged.

He never seemed to have a job and was constantly in debt to other people.

He has green eyes and jet-black hair that he kept long, even after the nineties ended and grunge was no longer fashionable.

He self-medicated with pot and other drugs before he was medicated for real when I was about fourteen.

He hit a girlfriend years after he and I stopped speaking, but she dropped the charges.

He was often verbally abusive to women.

He is on the child sex offender registry in South Australia, which has the strictest laws in the country for those types of crimes.

He was born in 1971.

Some of these things I know from him. Some I know from the police after I reported his abuse, and some from the internet. I once knew many more things about him, but my memory only gives me fragments now. It comes back to me in broken scenes.

I don't experience time like you do, or at least some of you do. My days can be punctuated by vivid memories.

One moment I am sitting in my parents' living room looking out the window at their jungle of a garden and the eucalypts beyond. Then, for a fraction of a second, the scene flicks. It's 1995, my childhood bedroom, and a man with long dark hair is looking through the window.

Until I started learning about trauma, I didn't know that there are some people for whom time moves only in one direction.

Trauma rewires the brain, almost changing us from the molecular level up. I used to think that I could emerge untouched from traumatic events, or at the very least that recovery was some kind of destination. That once I'd reached it, I would be whomever I was going to be had things not been so terribly interrupted.

But traumatic events produce profound and lasting changes in our minds, bodies, nervous system and memories. They touch every part of us. They change us.

We don't come back the same. We can't.

When I think about David, or when an image or sensation unexpectedly interrupts the flow of my day, sometimes I am in my body. But sometimes I am watching from the edge of the room. This is because traumatic memories are not encoded like ordinary memories – neat and ordered, brought to heel by a linear understanding of events. 'Integrated', as the technical term goes, into the rest of our lives.

While survivors will often force linearity onto stories of trauma, particularly written accounts, in an effort to explain them, this is not the embodied *experience* of trauma. Experiencing trauma, living trauma, means time collapses.

It runs in circles, then suddenly skips.

Two moments become one.

One moment stretches out before you like a highway through the desert – on and on until the horizon.

At times, there can be a memory – an image – that should make you cry, but instead you feel nothing. Sometimes someone touches you in a particular way, and you feel everything, and you don't know why.

Traumatic memories have, as the famous trauma therapist Judith Herman explains in *Trauma and Recovery*, a kind of 'frozen wordless' quality to them. They lack context, they lack narrative. They are pure sensation or image. Traumatic memories are fragments, not fully formed stories.

I will tell you the story of David and me. Or, rather, the story of David, my mother and me. But I will tell it in the only way I can.

Imagine I have taken my life, divided it into scenes – like a play – and made a deck of cards. Each card has a different scene, a different memory, or perhaps just a sensation. Imagine I then shuffle these cards. Place them on the table and take one off the top, then another and another until the table is scattered with them. A series of rooms laid out before you.

Eventually, as more cards are revealed, you might see patterns, connections – a story emerging. But they don't come out in a neat order. And because of that, you see that some stories loop and twist, start where you think they should end. Or you may think you've reached the end only to find it is the middle.

That is trauma.

That is the story of David, my mother and me.

―――

I met David on the now-archaic technology of 1990s online bulletin boards. Sometimes, on podcasts, I've heard people talk about these with nostalgia. A pre-internet internet where everyone you encountered lived in your town or city. At their height in America there were over 60,000 of them. In Australia, who knows? Some of them are still running in the United States, serving no greater purpose than to keep a piece of technological history alive. From the increased interest in them lately I suspect they may be falling into the realm of 'retro coolness'.

People who talk about bulletin boards – or 'BBSs' – with nostalgia don't see what I see. They don't know what I know. They talk about them as a funny nerdy phenomenon of the nineties where kids or adults who liked computers would talk or play games.

I think of them as the start of a previously unknown threat. A place where predators could reach through phone wires into the bedrooms of children and – as we now have the word to describe – 'groom' them.

BBSs had the added guarantee that the child you were talking to was local, within reach.

My parents bought me a subscription to a bulletin board. After watching a family friend type to girls her own age on the bulletin board, my parents thought that writing to others would help with my dyslexia, immersing me in language. They didn't comprehend what it was they had bought me a subscription to.

How could they? How could anyone know that this was the start of a whole new attack upon children? Completely unregulated, largely unknown to police. The perfect criminal apparatus masquerading as simple, harmless, human connection over an innocuous medium – a basic command line interface where people could meet in 'chat rooms' and talk.

I had an old Apple Mac set up in my bedroom on a desk at the end of my single bed. I'd arranged it so I could lie on my stomach in bed, propped up on pillows, and read and type. My bedroom was tucked away on the bottom floor of a long narrow two-storey house surrounded by bushland. My parents and sister slept upstairs. When everyone had gone to bed, I would boot up the computer – with its iconic set of Apple chords – and wait for the world to open up in front of me. Here in these virtual rooms was freedom; I was touching the outside.

Each room contained a different collection of people to meet. Each offered up a space where I might matter. And in time, I would discover private rooms – where David and I would meet and build our secrets.

While my parents couldn't have known the world that they had bought me a ticket to, or its dangers, there *were* people, or in my case a person, who knew what this new technology was allowing. BBSs had to be overseen. Every BBS had a SysOp: a system operator. SysOps could view any conversation occurring in any chat room on their bulletin board. A SysOp is God in the miniscule world of a BBS: all-knowing, all-powerful. Able to boot you off the system, revoke memberships, intercept, join or interrupt any conversation.

All-seeing, all-knowing, the SysOps must have been aware of what people like David were using his BBS for. I held a lot of anger at that SysOps for a long time. If I'm honest, I still do. It's easier to be angry with a person who could have stepped in and stopped something – helped you – when they play no other role in your life. It isn't as confusing as 'mother'.

But the SysOps did nothing. Perhaps he understood the business ramifications of reporting what was occurring on his BBS to the police. Perhaps he just didn't give a shit. This seems more likely – after all, he could simply have revoked the memberships of people who preyed on children. Either way, I've always thought there should be a special place in hell for that man.

Maybe I'm misdirecting some of my anger.

———

I can't tell you everything about the story of David and me. A series of scenes and feelings, in no particular order.

I used to think that because I didn't remember much – because it had dissolved into the general thrum of my life – I must be healed. Now I understand that not remembering is a sign of damage, not healing. That simple fact in itself has taken many years to understand.

I can tell you that David and I talked over the bulletin board for some time in our private room before we met in person. And I know that even after we had met face to face, after his girlfriend drove him to meet me outside my house, that I resisted any sexualisation of our conversations, though he would try.

He began by telling me things about him and his girlfriends: conversations, maybe the odd mention or comment about their sex life. Like when he had sex with a woman he was seeing in front of a friend who was a virgin, supposedly at her request.

Later, he would suggest things he wanted to do to me. Still, there remained an invisible barrier between us, between the talking and the acting, as though he were noble for restraining himself:

'I better not see you. The mood I'm in tonight, if I saw you, I'd have your legs wrapped around my face.'

This is what grooming looks like. It's the gradual weaving of sexual ideas into an otherwise normal conversation until they *become* the normal conversation. And then, slowly, inexorably, things move beyond conversation.

And yes, his girlfriend drove him to meet a twelve-year-old girl in the middle of the night. He didn't have a licence to drive himself. I have no earthly idea why she agreed to do this. Or why, one night, they came and collected me, put me to sleep in my clothes – jeans and a green-and-pink-striped t-shirt – on an old mattress with no sheets, only a dirty blanket, in the downstairs living room of his 1960s cream-brick apartment, while they slept together upstairs in his single bed. Then drove me home at 6 am, having exchanged no more than five sentences.

I spoke to her briefly, that girlfriend, while writing this. It was an attempt to put the fragments together in a way that made some sort of sense. 'I'm sorry for my part in this,' she said. Listening to her speak I realised she too was a victim of sorts – at the whim of his desires, his manipulation. She too struggled to break free of him, was used by him – for sex, for transport, money. As her first relationship, his toxin has flowed through her life too. But that is not my story to tell.

———

He would tell me about others, all of them under sixteen. Some were girlfriends, others a one-off encounter – though there's no doubt considerable effort on his part went into achieving that one encounter.

None of them stayed around as long as I did. Or, rather, none of them stayed around as long as he kept me around. While they came and went, I stayed.

I remained his secret. And he, in return, remained mine.

David would tell me what was wrong with all his girlfriends, and what was right about me. Our little conspiracy. In time we moved from talking over the computer to talking over the phone. Long conversations that would start after my parents went to bed and go all night. Building more conspiracies.

I would disconnect my modem and plug in an old phone, lying in my single bed, among poster-covered walls, the heat of the handset warming my face like the sun.

One night I went upstairs to get a drink of water while he waited on the end of the line in my bedroom. On my way back down the stairs I knocked a great big wooden tray my mother used for pens and pencils and other odds and ends. It had been sitting precariously at the top of the staircase, and in the dark I hit it with my foot. It crashed down a full flight of wooden stairs, the slate floors amplifying the already enormous noise even more.

'What on earth did you just do?!' David said through tears of laughter, imitating the crashing noises he'd heard through the phone.

I told him.

'And your parents just slept through that?!'

His laughter was infectious. We cried and snorted and laughed so much we could barely say a word, all the while nervous that someone would pick up the phone, having been woken by the ungodly racket.

Our fear that someone would pick up another phone and hear us wasn't unfounded. My parents did suspect I was talking to someone. We'd hear a click, and we would go silent, then quickly hang up. But come morning, no one in my family said a word to me. One time my parents disconnected the phone line in my bedroom, which was only there because the room was originally intended as a home office. After my parents went to bed, I dug a pair of pliers out of a drawer full of odds and ends in the living room, and carefully rewired the wall connection. When they hid the phone I had been using, I found an old dial-up one in the shed.

In retrospect, so many things about David and me were brazen. All the while my parents and I engaged in a strange game of mutual subterfuge. Looking back, a conversation with the son of long-time friends of my parents comes to mind. We were in our late teens and he was talking about his girlfriend, whom he was sleeping with. How he didn't need to sneak around: 'Gem, my parents aren't like yours. If they're going to have the thought, they just *have* the thought.'

It must have taken a lot of denial not to see that something was amiss in that house beyond normal adolescent rebellion.

I can't really tell you many details of what we said on those long nights. Ultimately they don't matter – likes, dislikes, lies and persuasion.

I only recall the incident of the wooden tray and the stairs so vividly because for some reason it still nearly makes me break into uncontrollable laughter. Maybe it's a funny story. Or maybe I've laughed off so many unfunny things in the context of 'family' that I have the ability to do the same with David.

Besides talking about the girlfriends, and everything that was wrong with them – they wore make-up to bed, which made them pathetic, or they weighed too much for his liking – there was also attentiveness to my loneliness. I relished the attention – that someone so worldly would dedicate hours and hours to speaking to me every night about my day, my life, my world. It was seductive to someone who felt alone and unheard.

I remember once saying that the thought of my parents dying made me cry and David being shocked and disbelieving. I don't know if I projected that level of disdain towards them or whether he fostered it.

No doubt he made jokes, usually at the expense of others. I probably laughed. But he wasn't funny. He was a mess.

I guess at the time he was excitement and flattery. When I met him he felt like vibrant colour.

Mostly, when I think back now, he was unremarkable. Beige.

―――

The windows of my childhood home, where David and I often met, were as good as doors. The whole front of our house was full-length glass. Large sections had no curtains or blinds, leaving those inside feeling exposed to anyone outside. The property backed on to an old private botanic garden, bushland and a mostly disused quarry. We had no fences around that house; nothing to keep me in or keep anyone else out.

The windows also ran floor-to-ceiling, and wound open outwards. A few quick tugs at four small pins and the screens popped out, leaving nothing but a chain tethering the wooden frame of the glass to the house.

Now predators could reach into my bedroom not only through the phone lines, but also through a door.

I moved out of that place when I was nineteen, a few years after my parents moved to Canberra. My mother was so sad about selling that house; to her it was perfect. High up in the treetops of a steep gully, with a creek at the bottom. It was beautiful. But for me, that beauty was lost – like so many things – to memories of David. Ridding ourselves of that house completely made me feel like I might finally begin to be safe.

When my family talks about it, they joke about the windows, and the myriad ways you could always get into and out of the place; it had seven doors to the outside, not including the window-doors. Later, as older teenagers, my sister and I made liberal use of these entries and exits, like teenagers do. Now we're adults this has become a safe topic of conversation and something my parents and sister can laugh about. I play along, but the conversation makes me queasy.

For me, there was nothing safe, nothing funny, about how easily I could slip unnoticed from that house into the night. And in those conversations, it strikes me again how deeply my mother can bury her secrets within herself.

———

I remember our first kiss. My first kiss. We had been out driving around the city with another friend from the bulletin board. Me feeling reckless and cool, escaping into the night in my purple Doc Martens boots and plaid miniskirt.

David and I slid back into my bedroom through one of those window-doors. This one opened into the spare room, which was downstairs in my little kingdom – where no one sleeping upstairs could hear. A large room, with a queen-sized bed in the middle.

I don't know if we talked, though I'm sure we did – aimlessly and meaninglessly. I do remember him leaning over me, laying me back on the bed with me still wearing my Doc Martens boots. I do know he kissed me, his tongue in my mouth, sliding past my teeth and over my own tongue to the back of my mouth, tasting like cigarettes. And that years later he told me through laughter it had been a terrible kiss.

———

There are only a few other images from that time that are still vivid enough for me to recall with any clarity. I'm sure my police statement from sixteen years ago would unearth many long-forgotten details. For now, if my mind needs to keep a few things secret, I'm going to let it. There's enough reality to deal with without going looking for more. Or maybe there's more of my mother in me than I would like to admit.

So, I have fragments:

One night, watching a brawl in a car park down below, safe beside him in his single bed in the dark we watched through broken venetian blinds, the traffic streaming by on the highway. I'd never seen a fist fight before. I'd never felt protected like I did in that moment with him; safe from the violence below, not realising that the violence was in that very room with me.

Him at a girls' sleepover party I was attending, coming through someone else's window-door. I talked my friends into inviting him over. We stole money from my friend's mother's purse to cover his taxi fare because he couldn't afford his own. He, two of my young friends and I went for a walk around the suburban blocks of the inner-eastern suburbs of Adelaide. Past bluestone houses and brush fences. Well-kept parks with the obligatory set of swings and slippery dip. We girls in our pyjamas, he in pants and a button-up linen shirt. As we crossed a road, I was about to step off a high gutter in the dark in bare feet. He caught me under the arms and lifted me, letting me land gently on my feet on the bitumen. Like I weighed nothing. I was twelve; I probably did weigh nothing. It gave me such a rush to have someone touch me like that – to carry me over a minor peril to safety.

Watching *Rage* on ABC-TV at two in the morning in the spare room of my parents' house, Garbage playing in the background, him reaching over and kissing me. Taking my hand around the wrist and placing it on his erect cock and whispering, 'You don't have to do anything, I just want you to know that it's there.' Falling asleep to the sound of nineties grunge and waking hours later, the TV now off, to feel David trying to reach under my clothes and into my underwear. Me silently removing his hand. A small act of resistance.

Us in my bedroom, he having slid through the window-door. Me wearing emerald green satin pyjama pants my grandparents gave me, lying in bed on top of the covers. Him whispering in my ear, 'I want to make you orgasm.' Defiant, I said, 'No, I won't let you,' without even knowing what an orgasm was. I said it so loudly, but not a word left my mouth. He got his wish. Fear and pleasure cohabiting in one body, control in someone else's.

Much later, me lying again in his bed, my hand timidly extending towards his erection, not placed there this time but searching it out, a bulge I didn't understand. Quickly withdrawing my hand again.

Me in his apartment. That apartment, with its stale cigarettes and pot, dust and old coffee cups. How we walked in the front door, and always – always – straight upstairs to the bedroom.

I never wanted sexual attention as a child. I just wanted attention. I didn't really know what sex was. But I wanted to matter. And to David I seemed to matter.

In time, I gave up my small acts of resistance. I stopped saying no to touching, to orgasms . . . to anything else he wanted. My resistance artfully, gently, worn down. I welcomed him through that window-door.

I said yes, as much as a child can say yes to something they don't comprehend.

I said yes.

David and I continued our secret meetings through the nineties, from when I was twelve until I was fourteen, though with a brief reprieve in the middle. I know it all got too messy and hazy for me to remember much of it now, mostly from the alcohol. I know as I got older, he got more daring – he pushed me further, he got me drunk, he got me stoned. He took my virginity.

He'd moved to a new house by then, to an old single-storey semi-detached house not far from his old apartment. It was just as filthy and worn down as his last place, but with a small garden out the front. A girlfriend my age and I had caught a bus there, and he greeted us with a cheap bottle of rum. Later in the night, after much drinking and dancing, as my friend slept peacefully in his bed in the other room, he lay me back on his couch, still clothed. I remember clenching my eyes and face in pain, through the fog of booze – willing it all just to be over, but not raising my voice or hand in protest. There was something fated about it; of course he would get this in the end, even if it took him years.

Once he was done, he seemingly losing interest, and I stumbled through the apartment to the bathroom – past a round table stacked with dishes, into a laundry with a toilet at one end and a pile of dirty clothes the size of a couch at the other. Standing in the toilet, swaying, I mopped up blood with toilet paper.

When I returned to the couch, he said he was shocked it was my first time. I don't know what distorted image, what fantasised projection, he had of me to think that I would have slept with anyone by that age. Or maybe it had nothing to do with me. Maybe it was a lie he told himself to make his actions less appalling. A glimmer of a conscience or merely another act of degradation – who can say? I've given up trying to understand David's mind. I'm fairly sure he doesn't understand it – his grip on reality loosened with age, so the police and public prosecutor told me later; multiple suicide attempts, manic-depressive, incoherent statements and psychosis.

In all our encounters he never had an orgasm. I do not know what it says about what he was seeking, though I have wondered often.

———

We lost touch twice in this time. The first was when I was thirteen and he simply stopped answering my calls; the ones I made from my secret bedroom phone. Perhaps he found a new girl who held his attention better than me. I called for months and no one answered. I was no longer on Adam – my parents having finally cancelled my subscription. Eventually I put the phone away. I returned to my life before David – to school and girlfriends and the worry of homework.

I tried to forget him.

A year or more lapsed, and then he phoned me; he told me he missed me terribly – needed me in his life. That he thought of me constantly. My hands shook as I held the receiver to my ear. In the time that had passed I had become afraid of David. But the fear had not completely taken over;

deep in me I felt the lure of mattering. When I hung up the phone I thought about how he used to make me feel; how his time and attention could make a goddess of me, if only for a moment. And yes, I remembered the physical pleasure.

Our nightly phone calls resumed. Before I knew it, I was back in his bed. Only this time with drugs and alcohol; fear and pleasure still cohabiting in my body when we were together as they did when I was twelve, but the fear now outstripped the pleasure. This is when I lost my virginity to him, on that dirty couch.

The second time we drifted apart, it was me who lost interest, who pulled away. The fear had grown. The sense of wonder at his attention, of how it made me feel, had evaporated. With age, I saw him more plainly – I saw the mess. Still, I went along with it for a time, maybe six months, though I needed alcohol to be lured into his bed, to be near him at all. I suspect what I really craved was his offer of booze and its oblivion, rather than his company. But once sufficiently numbed, I rehearsed the same steps he had taught me when I was twelve – escalating with every encounter.

At my house one night he turned the light on in my bedroom to look for his watch, which he had dropped on the floor. For the first time ever he stood in front of me naked. In the bright light that we'd never before dared turn on – lest it wake my family, or break the spell he had woven.

I looked up at him from my single bed and drunkenly ridiculed him: 'You look hilarious naked.' Then I laughed. Nastily.

For the first time in all those hours we had spent together, I laughed *at* him, not with him. This skinny pale older man with a sad limp penis. I mocked him from my bed with my youthful unblemished skin, fit and toned from weekly sports training.

In that moment, when my mocking laugh cut the air, I think he realised he'd lost control of me. I couldn't be subjected to his whims anymore, even with alcohol.

I saw him.

He was furious. He dressed immediately and left, through my window-door. While I can't be sure, I suspect that was the last sexual encounter we ever had.

Soon after, I gravitated back to my school friends, away from him and alcohol – drawn in by the pressures of high school and good grades. I buried myself in building a future, placing him in a box and closing the lid . . . at least for a time.

You probably want to know more about David and me. About how he so deftly convinced me, and other girls, to do the things he wanted. There are gaps in my memory – in my life – that will never be filled. What I can tell you, though, is that the manipulation runs deep. So deep that you will protect your own attacker. You will want them and you will want them to want you. And so a young girl may phone her abuser for months hoping for an answer, long after he has moved on to other prey. They capture you in your entirety – from your body to your mind, and maybe, for a little while, your soul. Some people struggle to ever break free; to smash the illusion, as I finally did.

CHAPTER THREE

Things we don't talk about

You might be thinking by now, 'Not me, I would have told people as soon as I understood what had happened to me.' But you are wrong.

You will protect your attacker.

Far, far more often than not, and for extended periods of time, the abused will protect their abuser. In all manner of contexts.

Silence is the most powerful weapon in the abuser's arsenal. And they wield it so deftly; manipulating your personal weaknesses and fears, seeding doubts about authority figures, and playing on social discourses of shame and blame.

In my family, there was ample ammunition. There are many things we do not talk about, that we keep silent.

Difficult things. The reality of things. As though if we don't pay attention to them, they might just go away.

―

David never directly told me to keep us a secret. Instead he would insist that my parents and family didn't understand me. Only he understood me. Only he and his opinions mattered. His ex-girlfriend, who drove him to my house, told me he was proud of his relations with me (I refuse to call it a relationship). Boasted about it to others – told them I wanted it, was asking for it.

As Doreen St. Félix wrote on the sixtieth anniversary of *Lolita*: 'Lolita came to be a name for what are called sexually precocious girls but doting, pedophillic men did not come to be known as Humberts.'

He saw nothing wrong with coaxing a twelve-year-old girl into a sexual relationship, despite his ex-girlfriend and other friends chiding him. I'll never know why they didn't report him. Why they didn't take more serious action. But I guess, if I'm to be generous, at seventeen and eighteen they were barely more than children themselves.

If anything, I think he flirted with the danger of getting caught. Adelaide is a small town. Once, he bumped into a friend of our family at a party – the adult son of a colleague of my father that David somehow knew.

David told me he had mentioned me to this family friend, who said he knew me when I was a very young child. David, according to his telling, winked and said, 'She's all grown up now.' In my naivety, I laughed along with him – another part of our conspiracy.

Much later, perhaps as his mental state deteriorated further, he sent a detailed email to my father. Offering up his guilt to a man who most certainly would have brought down fatherly rage and justice.

Almost like history repeating – like a broken mirror – I intercepted the email and deleted it. I kept the abuse secret, as I knew my mother had done with the letters previously.

———

The most vivid dream I've ever had was about David. It was years later, sometime in my late twenties.

In the dream, he and I are sitting at a table in his first apartment – the one with the bedroom upstairs that overlooked the car park. My sister and mother are there too. My mother is at the head of the table, my sister and David opposite each other – I am seated next to David. The table in my dream was one he never owned, a formica number from the 1950s – the kind that eventually became vintage chic. It wasn't clear in the dream what had brought the four of us together, my mother chatting away like he was a friend. Just a normal conversation.

I was tense. I knew the situation was explosive, so many secrets sitting around that table threatening to bubble over. I didn't want them to, and I sat silently watching their conversation, hoping no one would figure out what was under the surface.

In my dream David reached out and combed his fingers through my hair. No one else noted this gesture or its intimacy. But in that touch was every ounce of fear and pleasure he had ever induced in me. That touch terrified me so much I woke up with adrenaline still coursing through me.

I can still feel it, whenever I think about that dream. Viscerally, like everything is happening all over again.

At the start, I wanted to keep it from my parents because I was ashamed. But later, when I realised that what had happened to me was not okay, that it had damaged me, I kept it from them because I sensed it was something they couldn't handle. More specifically, that my mother couldn't handle.

My mother is someone who many regard as 'having it together' – up-to-date on all the latest literature, political happenings. As she has grown older, she has always been on point, with trendy haircuts and 'edgy' clothing, as she likes to call it, though I've always hated that word: 'That's what old people say to try and sound like they're still with it, Mum,' I tell her.

She is not your typical mother, nor does she want to be. She has disdain for anyone who has allowed themself to become 'dowdy'; who allows themself to fall behind the times – aesthetically, intellectually.

Don't be fooled, though – this her papier-mâché armour.

There is a fragility, an emotional volatility and extreme sensitivity, just below the surface. One which made me sense – even at a young age – that the story of David and me was more than she could hold.

Or maybe this is what I've reconstructed as an adult to make sense of my actions. I just know that every fibre of me screamed, 'Do not tell her.' I am not alone. Australian research into sexual abuse estimates that as many as 80 per cent of children who are sexually abused do not disclose the abuse before adulthood.

At sixteen, I knew something wasn't right about what had happened between David and me. At the age when everyone else began their sexual exploration, I found myself depressed and shut off. I would date boys, ironically developing a bad reputation among my peers while never letting the boys near me. Meanwhile, other girls began practising what I had been shown at twelve with their fumbling – but appropriately aged – counterparts.

I asked my parents if I could see a psychologist. I was depressed and the only reason I could find for it seemed to lie in my past. Seeing psychologists was a fairly popular pastime for private school girls; the school even had one on staff – though I never quite trusted her, since she was part of the establishment. The first psychologist I saw urged me to tell my parents about David. She suggested that it was the only way to 'heal that little girl'.

She was wrong.

It wasn't safe to tell them. Telling would have put that little girl and that teenage girl in danger. My parents didn't even ask why I needed to see a psychologist. I doubt my honesty would have been met with the requisite compassion and contrition. My mother's suffering would have outstripped mine; that tilted ground sliding towards her and her matter yet again.

I feel vindicated now. The fact that I can tell this story now in such detail is because of the knowledge my mother will soon be dead. Now, twenty years later, it's finally safe. People, even psychologists, don't understand that the danger of someone like David is often intertwined with another type of danger: 'home'. Sometimes there are things we don't talk about for good reason.

I changed psychologists. This one didn't insist I tell my parents. Instead, she suggested I report David to the police.

I think the young can have a certain protective naivety at times; like that saying, 'a drunk in a car crash', they bounce. I didn't understand at sixteen and seventeen how hard it is to prosecute sexual crimes. In my mind, an injustice had been committed and it needed to be put right. When my psychologist said this could be done by going to the police – by pressing charges – I thought, 'Yes, we will correct this. And he will not hurt other girls. He won't get to live a normal life while others suffer.'

If I knew what I do now, about how the justice system treats women and sexual assault, I'm not sure I would have decided so quickly, almost simply, to proceed. Though I would still have pursued it in the end; justice – or, more specifically, injustice – has always been a driving force in my life. My entire professional existence pivots on trying to alleviate inequality and poverty – I see a great injustice in human suffering and feel compelled to try and stop it.

My psychologist shepherded me through the court system, protecting me from its harsher edges without me realising. She came to police stations; she came to hearings. Later, I learnt she even went to David's house with the police when they went to collect his computer and all its files. She eviscerated him with language, telling him never to come near me again. She didn't need to do that; there was already a restraining order in place. I suspect she did a great many things behind the scenes she didn't need to do, to make the wheels of justice run smoothly without much input from me.

Occasionally a force comes along that does even out the weight of the bad in our lives, at least a little.

———

Reflecting now on the ways in which I wanted or tried to say no but was artfully worn down and silenced for so long, I realise we have only recently begun to teach children and young adults about the intricacies of consent.

Again, this has been triggered by defiant women speaking out – through art, through writing – about rampant sexual assault. This time on university campuses in America. The most memorable of these is Emma Sulkowicz's performance artwork, 'Carry that Weight'. In 2014 Sulkowicz carried a 23-kilogram mattress everywhere she went on the Columbia University campus for a full semester and even to her graduation ceremony.

It was the mattress she was raped on.

I was walking with a friend through the Canberra bush one afternoon soon after my mum got sick. Kicking along the red dirt tracks of Mount Majura, we talked about how our ideas on consent had changed. A man from my friend's past had recently apologised to her for what he now realised was a breach of consent. She was so taken aback – both by the fact she hadn't realised it was a breach of consent until he apologised, and that he had volunteered the apology. Perhaps we really are in the midst of a profound social shift?

At a recent dinner party of peers, my friend explained that everyone at the party realised that at no point in their education did anyone explain consent. 'No,' I replied. 'Never. But it all seems so obvious now.' Still, no one ever tried to empower us to decide and act on who could and could not touch our bodies. As we talked, I realised it's almost as though we were set up to be victims – never given the skills to protect ourselves. It still lingers, this lack of empowerment, of boundaries. Knowing is not the same as enacting.

In her book *The First Stone* Helen Garner describes a moment when a stranger kissed her violently on a train and she froze, allowing him to continue. When I read that passage, I immediately recalled dozens of times in my life when my body, my being, had been violated and my response was not to make a scene. To let the moment pass, as Garner did.

Not long after reading Garner's book, in my late twenties while living in Brunswick, I sat at Anstey train station waiting to catch a train to the city. Looking off into the middle distance, an elderly Italian man sat down on the bench next to me. He asked the time, then began caressing my bare arm. 'I don't know,' I said, as his hand settled on the skin of my thigh, just above my knee. He smelt of tobacco and sweat, in the summer sun. I was appalled, repelled, deeply uncomfortable. And yet, as I stood up to walk away, I heard myself apologise.

The only difference between this and events from earlier in my life was the anger I felt at myself for doing exactly what is expected of women in these situations. To swallow the injustice. To not speak.

CHAPTER FOUR

All the broken pieces

On what we understood to be our last Christmas with my mother, I was searching around my parents' house for a stapler. I found one that had been around since my childhood, sitting on the desk in my father's study just off the living room. Its survival was quite the feat, given my parents had moved city, moved house, then moved and moved again. But here was this stapler, at least twenty years old.

It didn't work. My father, standing behind me as I threw it in the bin, muttered quietly to me, 'In this house you keep dead things, detritus. Old pens that don't work, bits of paper and broken crap, until it rusts and decays.'

Do secrets decay?

The running joke in our family is that things have been 'cleaned up'. 'Cleaned up' is a euphemism for 'put haphazardly in a place known only to my mother' – to resurface in days, years or never.

Has my past been cleaned up too?

The disorder of my parents' house escalated as my mother's cancer did, and as the chemotherapy drugs obliterated her mind. One time, in that year of my mother's cancer, I unearthed a new pair of bathers I'd bought. They were wedged between stacks of ancient *New Yorker* magazines, in a box in a room at the very end of their rambling Canberra house.

All the broken pieces put in containers, stacked into drawers and cupboards, giving the illusion of a house in order. Any attempts to create real order were read as criticisms – everything is fine, just don't look in the drawer, in the box. Just don't look too closely. At anything. And so the illusion is maintained.

I continue to watch my father trying to live a life – to keep on top of all the things my mother is gradually dropping, from bills to house maintenance, because of her illness – in the midst of this illusion of order. What does it say about this man, about this woman, that challenging this illusion is worse than living within the chaos it creates?

———

I have told my mother she is dying five times.

I don't think that's something many people do even once in their life. But with every new stage of her cancer I come like some kind of angel of death to deliver the news. In the months immediately following her diagnosis the bad news kept coming. Not just the breast but the lymph and the bones. Not just the bones, the brain. Soon after the brain, the liver.

As a matter of course, and choice, I received all her medical reports and scans before she did. Placing her needs above my own, I would bring them to her. We would sit at the large family dining table – the centre of their home – and hold a meeting. A series of family cancer meetings.

I would bring with me all the research I could gather on what options and potential pathways lay ahead, and we would lay them out – physically and metaphorically – on that big table and talk about what to do.

It made me sick to do it. Literally sick. I would deliver the news, I would retreat, then spend five days in bed with a cold. Every time. No matter the wreckage, I did my duty.

Why? She wanted to know before she saw the doctors so she could ask the right questions, so she could be assertive and not fall to pieces. And so it was, I sacrificed myself, my health, at the altar of my mother's matter and my father's helplessness, even though I suspect it made very little difference to how her medical appointments proceeded.

Of course, there has to be a deeper reason why I was compelled to do it, this daughterly duty.

Maybe I did it because whenever we had the 'you're dying' conversation, there would be a moment when all the bullshit fell away. A moment when the denial and the secrets that fortified her life were gone. Just a brief moment. Maybe a day if I was lucky. Suddenly, there I was, talking to her – really talking to her – about what was truly happening. Despite the horror of the situation it was seductive – that flicker of acceptance that yes, she did have cancer; the flicker of a rational mind, of love. Then gone.

When my mother was diagnosed with advanced inflammatory breast cancer, just eight months after I moved from Melbourne to Canberra, where my parents live, my husband and I moved in with my parents.

At the time, I said to myself that I wanted to be there for her in all the ways she had never been there for me. But there is another reason that I was willing to take up the mantle of truth teller. I could be strong and honest where she was frightened and trapped in denial. That is to say, I could find a way of being in the world other than that which she had showed me.

It sounds so altruistic. But my husband and I were also building a house and we had nowhere to live. My mother said, 'Move in, I'll give you the second wing of the house. It will be all yours, your own bathroom and everything.' It is a beautiful house, the front end the 'family space' with a study and my parents' bedroom attached. The back end has a large bedroom with its own bathroom, overlooking a rambling garden that leads on to a bush reserve.

We bought the line 'It will be all yours', and we moved in.

My husband only lasted a month, decamping quickly to couch-surf, or to house-sit on the other side of town. His leaving was the beginning of the end; our marriage would not prove strong enough to survive my mother's dying. I believe he did not want to live in the midst of my mother's slow death, his own mother having survived breast cancer earlier in our marriage. Nor did he want to watch his wife stare down monsters from her past, while she cared for a woman he could never see as more than a monster herself – my mother. And so he left me, physically and emotionally, to face the onslaught of disease and memories. I remained in my parents' house with our dog, my sick mother and my quietly concerned father, believing that my staying might finally heal old wounds.

And there were moments when it almost felt like it could. The night the radiologist rang at 11 pm to tell us my mother had a large metastatic brain tumour, we sat at the family dining table and drank whisky, ate expensive cheese. We said, 'Screw it all,' and we cried – together. That night I snuck up from the back of the house and crawled into bed beside her. Feeling the heavy weight of her body next to me, I fell asleep in her warmth, feeling like I had 'family', like I knew what 'mother' was.

The time we used her cancer to take down the king and queen of our local dog park. Often, there was a black-and-white cattle dog that grabbed the collars of other dogs at that park, strangling them. No dog had died from one of these calculated attacks, but it was probably only a matter of time. None of the regulars quite knew how to bring it up with the owners, who had established themselves at the top of the social hierarchy. Dog parks are deeply political places. There are alliances, rituals, and always the chance you might get voted off the island.

Rather than confront the owners, people began to take their dogs' collars off before coming to the park. To add a good dollop of awkwardness to the situation, the dog belonged to my boss.

My mother has always had a certain sense of justice, of the way things should be. She'd been plotting to get that dog out of the park, or at least muzzled, for months. One afternoon she said, 'You know, I've noticed people don't like talking back to cancer patients.' And with that, a plan was hatched.

I drove down to the park with my great big Bernese Mountain Dog – Mabel – and my mother, bald head on full display despite the winter air. When the dog and its owner arrived, she was ready. She walked directly up to the man and delivered her lines with an I-will-shame-the-shit-out-of-you kind of tirade. It was excruciatingly awkward to watch, with her making as big a scene as she possibly could. Emboldened by the fact someone had finally raised the issue, others joined in, nodding furiously as she waved her finger in his face, her large beaded necklace jangling with each word and exaggerated movement of her arms. 'You're lucky your dog hasn't been reported and put down. How can you live with yourself, bringing it here without a muzzle? I saw it nearly kill a puppy last week. Don't think I won't report you!' I stood on the sidelines making 'what am I supposed to do? she has cancer' shrugs at my boss.

Back in the car we laughed hard. 'Did you see his face? He didn't know what to do! Getting shouted down by a cancer patient in the middle of a park. We got him!'

'Well done, Mum,' I said, chuckling, enjoying her triumph.

Then there was the day that Donald Trump was elected. We gathered again around my parents' dining room table in the evening – a table built to withstand decades of intellectual and political debate, not just medical decision-making. We sat there, family and family friends – other academics – dumbfounded, desolate.

'It will all be okay, he won't last, this whole situation is ridiculous. He'll be impeached before you know it.'

Her words were soothing, they acted like a balm. Only later did I think to myself: 'Of course you can offer platitudes; you won't have to live in the world he creates.'

———

In time that wing of the house we were offered became a room – my mother entering at will. I would come home from work to find that all the furniture had been rearranged. One time, a brand-new bed appeared that took up so much space I couldn't even walk around it to get in at night. I had to launch myself into bed Superman-style.

As well as all the possessions I needed to survive the twelve months while our house was built, the room already contained two heavy antique chests of drawers that used to belong to my grandparents. To this I added another two. One wall was already taken up by a floor-to-ceiling cupboard. As the months passed, more objects filled 'my' space – furniture and things my mother bought me for my new house – along with memories and betrayal.

The room was closing in on me, physically and emotionally.

When I walked in one day to find her pulling my belongings out of the big cupboard to 'organise them', I finally snapped. I walked out to the garage, took a green bike lock I'd just bought for my bike, and locked the cupboard door. If I had no other space in the world that belonged to me, by hell I was going to have that cupboard.

The cupboard incident, as I now refer to it – or the creeping invasion of privacy, and the general insanity of the situation – was exacerbated by the drugs. They gave her steroids for the brain tumour, and afterwards for the chemo. The steroids made her psychotic. Sometimes the psychosis came in the form of a rapid dismantling of some part of the house, which others had to reassemble later. Furniture appeared and demanded to be assembled; other furniture disappeared. One day, a whole wardrobe was dismantled on command – my father getting smaller and more tired running after her and the endless stream of dis-assemblage and assemblage.

It was the illusion of order against the disorder of cancer. All the broken organs, bones and lymph system put inside the container of her body, then placed inside a house. Holding her world together with denial.

Often, the psychosis took the form of yelling, as when I was a child. At times the world shrunk to the size of that cupboard and me, with my dying mother yelling insults at me through a psychotic haze. The psychosis didn't change her, it merely intensified her most negative parts; you do not matter, you have *no matter*. Even as an adult you will be denied a two-by-two metre of space to call your own.

Even when my personal world was invaded in the name of 'helping', like the times she foraged through my bedroom in my youth, it was not the protective act of a parent. It was an assault on the idea that I matter.

―

Through the worst of her drug-induced psychosis and the yelling, my father watched. Silent.

I asked him what gave him the right to throw his daughter in front of that rage to save himself. It may have been the most honest and fierce thing I have ever said to him. He did not reply. My only triumph: the guilt of his turned back. He was unable to meet my eyes.

One night, sitting at the dining table, I tried to explain to my mother how she'd been rude to my husband earlier that day, in as gentle but assertive a manner as I could manage. She stormed off to her bedroom crying. Hours later, I snuck up to their room and put my ear to the bedroom wall. I could hear my mother sobbing, frantically asking my father, 'Why aren't you on my side?!'

I didn't hear a reply.

And then I understood. He was on no one's side. Or, more accurately, he was on his own side.

As I retreated back to my room, I wondered whether he would have stayed silent if those letters had come to *his* attention twenty years before. I'd like to believe not. My father may be a coward in the face of my mother's emotions, but he has never been one in the world at large. I don't believe he would have been silent. But he too has lived in this house, this family, which looks orderly but has so much turbulence underneath the surface. To some degree, he also chose not to lift the lid of many boxes.

CHAPTER FIVE

A year of cancer

There are things we are not allowed to admit. Just before my mother got sick, I read Meghan Daum's 'Matricide' from her collection of essays, *The Unspeakable*. Even then it struck a chord, as though foreshadowing the next year of my life. Speaking what the title of the book implies is an 'unspeakable' truth, Daum writes about her impatience with her mother's death. More than that, her indifference.

We are meant to plead for more time when our family members become ill. But not all of us do. More importantly, perhaps, not all of us should.

Early on in my mother's illness, I did what I suspect most people do. I grieved for the impending loss and I hoped for something profound to occur. I waited for a connection to form. For us to look one another in the eye and realise: *It has come to this. This is our final chance to undo the damage*. We would speak of those letters and everything that happened and that didn't happen but should have.

I was swiftly disabused of these expectations.

A friend who works in palliative care told me one night, over drinks and sympathy, 'People die the way they live.' My mother's denial about her own dying, about her own life, made it clear that we would not be doing any excavation of our relationship. Secrets were going to stay secret – hers and mine, and the ones that bound us.

This is my almost-unspeakable truth: with every test and every scan, I hoped for bad news. And then bad news came, and came, followed by waves of grief and inevitable guilt as I delivered that bad news to her. Sitting calmly at the dining room table and saying, 'You are dying,' over and over. You have cancer in your bones: *you are dying*. You have cancer in your brain: *you are dying*. You have cancer in your liver and the chemotherapy isn't working: *I really mean it, you are dying*.

Then the waves of guilt would pass, and I would breathe: 'Let this be over soon.'

I could cope with travelling along on the same tired tracks of our life before the cancer, our fractured lie of 'mother' and 'daughter'. But living with cancer isn't living; it's knowing that you are dying. This creates a type of ambiguity that is no doubt difficult to endure, but which I personally have found intolerable to be privy to. To be part of. It is what anthropologists call the liminal phases of our lives – the points where we are between two more stable states of being.

It hollowed me out. I began to become my mother's illness – turning in on myself, letting my life stand still while I watched cancer move forward. I tracked it in every scan and blood test, holding my breath for the months in between. I knew every progression of her cancer before she did, just as she had known I was abused before I could.

I abandoned myself for the sake of 'family'.

———

For most of that year of cancer, I oscillated between grief, anger and numbness. Her illness brought old ghosts and secrets to the surface in new ways – I turned inwards in an attempt to sort through the fragments. And how those fragments intermingled with the present, where my mother's psychotic haze produced harsh words, often about me not caring enough about her or for her.

My personal favourite: the day she called me a martyr. On the day of the now infamous cupboard incident, my mother – who took every hurt that was ours and made it her own – called me a martyr.

I wasn't always contrite in the face of her onslaught. Sometimes I walked away and hid. Sometimes I fired back as good as I got. On other days, I responded to her as you would a child – 'That's not a very nice thing to say, you know' – shaming her into better behaviour. I'd been using that tactic for several years before we knew about the cancer and the psychosis that treatment brought.

I figured if she had the emotional age of a thirteen-year-old, accordingly I would assume the role of parent and speak to her as if she were a child. It worked well, but it didn't always hold up in the face of the drugs and illness. And I couldn't always muster the patience to deploy it. That particular day, the day of the cupboard incident, wrapping my bike lock around the door handles and locking it, I pushed my heart through gritted teeth: 'Well that's a fucking ironic thing to say.'

Months later, swimming in the ocean south of Canberra where my family have spent nearly every summer of my life, my sister and I talked about our mother's martyrdom between ducking under waves. My sister had been making routine trips back from America to visit, ever since our mother was diagnosed.

We were swimming beneath a cliff with houses perched on top. The coast along this part of New South Wales is lined with dense subtropical bush. Here, in our spot, the bush almost kisses the ocean. We've come to this place – this sanctuary full of birds, cicadas and the occasional wallaby – all our lives, no matter where we happened to be living at the time, even if it meant a sixteen-hour drive.

A year of cancer

On this day, like so many we have spent here, my sister and I had the whole beach to ourselves. Just us and the ocean, with the houses looking down on us from above.

Earlier, my mother had told us that when we were kids, she had rented one of those houses, she and her best friend with their four children between them.

'Wasn't I a good mother? Walking up and down all those hundreds of stairs to the beach each day with you kids,' she'd said.

As we dived and swam and floated in the ocean, looking back at those winding staircases up to the top of the cliff, my sister said: 'She thinks that's what made her a good mother. Doing things she didn't like, that she chose to do, made her a good mother.' I nodded, 'Yes.'

We never asked her to do those things. We asked for other things. We asked for safety. We asked for the right kind of silence. The silence of peace, not the silence of betrayal.

Somewhere, deep within herself, she knows all this. It is why she feels the need to recite fairly ordinary acts of parenting and say, 'See? I was a good mother.' Good mothers, I suspect, don't need to do that.

———

Sometimes, in that year of cancer, I threw reality at her when she least expected it. One evening, as the four of us shared dinner, she began telling a favourite story of hers – a story about me. 'When you were little you would never let us hug, you'd push into the middle of us.' A child who was so needy she couldn't let her parents show affection without including her, my mother's tone implied. As she laughed, I replied, expressionless, 'That's because I didn't feel secure and loved as a child.'

The room went silent. The type of uneasy silence that arises when someone has broken an unspoken social rule, disrupting the natural order of things.

Another time over dinner, when my parents were musing about my father's sister – who was derided as a crazy narcissist and 'wild' in the least complimentary sense of the word – I reminded them that when I was a child they would tell me I was like her. Taken aback, my mother said, 'It was meant to be a deterrent,' then added uncertainly, 'I think.'

'How can it be a deterrent when I never met her?' I said.

'Oh.' Then an awkward change in subject.

My sister thinks that they simply couldn't understand me, so they pegged me to the closest female relative that I physically resembled. But tell a child they're bad enough times and they will embody it; they will become bad because that is the slot in the family structure where you have placed them, that you have made available to them. And here again, family stories interweave with societal narratives which we have still not fully torn down: only bad girls are sexually abused; they must have asked for it in some way; they are 'wild'. They are to blame.

I *was* wild. I was wildly trying to rebuild what was around me into something that I needed – tearing at their denial with my reality from the earliest of ages. Wildly trying to matter. There is a passage in Maggie O'Farrell's memoir *I Am, I Am, I Am* that reminds me a great deal of my younger self, and maybe even a little of my adult self:

> I have this compulsion for freedom, for a state of liberation. It is an urge so strong, so all-encompassing that it overwhelms everything else. I cannot stand my life as it is. I cannot stand to be here, in this town, in this school. I have to get away . . . and only then can I create a life that will be liveable for me. I may appear flighty and capricious, talking to you one day, retreating the next but, you see, I have to concentrate everything on freeing myself and nothing can get in my way. I cannot bear for anything or anyone to slow me down, distract me, fetter me.

From the outside, I imagine, this can look a little wild.

―

In the year of cancer, my verbal throwing of reality and truth had an unnerving effect on the house – the 'family' – that denial built. Now I wasn't just her truth teller of cancer; I was the truth teller of all things hidden and secret. I was dangerous and, as the year moved on, my mother avoided conversations and situations that might exceed mere pleasantries.

But for most of that year I turned in on myself. It was the year I finally broke open, and with my own hands dug out all that was rotten.

I'd lie in bed in that room at the end of the house, sometimes alone, sometimes curled up with my back to my husband. A few times I'd try to reach out and tell him what she had said that day, or how it was weaving itself into and around the fragments of other memories, memories of David.

He would listen; he would be sad and angry with me and for me, and try to be there for me. But, ultimately, he was unable to comprehend the depth of my sadness or the way that time – more than ever – had ceased to be linear. I was a twelve-year-old girl alone; I was a thirty-two-year-old woman whose mother was dying. I was both these things at once, and all the confusion of the twenty years that lay between them.

For all anyone might have tried, I turned in on myself that year. I left him and others even though I was often right beside them. Some work, some excavating, must be done alone.

I didn't lack compassion for my mother's response to her illness, but I did lack understanding. Three years before I let myself become absorbed into my mother's illness, I was life-threateningly ill myself – and I responded very differently.

While living in Melbourne, at the end of completing

my PhD, I was struck by Guillain-Barré syndrome, an autoimmune condition that, after a flu and in times of prolonged stress, causes your nervous system to forget which parts are virus and which parts are body. Killing the virus, your body shreds the nerves; confused, it does not know which bits matter. It was as though I'd absorbed my upbringing at a cellular level – my body working hard to destroy its own matter.

My disease is far better known these days because of its link to the Zika virus that began with mosquitoes in Brazil and threatened to become a pandemic in 2015. While Zika was most widely feared for its effects on unborn babies – leaving them with life-threatening birth defects – it also causes GBS, and there are now more cases worldwide than ever before.

The illness left me debilitated and in constant pain: twenty-four-hour-a-day pain. The only way I have ever been able to convey that pain since is to say that, at its worst, I would idly daydream of having my hands amputated. Surely that would be less painful than keeping them attached to my body.

I couldn't walk, couldn't hold a plate or a cup. I couldn't bear the pain of being touched or hugged. But I was lucky; it didn't go to my heart or my lungs. My body realised just in time that I mattered.

Nearly four years on, I'm still recovering. Most mornings I wake with a tingling pain in my hands and my whole nervous system buzzing as though with electricity. I wonder whether, if someone touched me in those moments, my skin would be vibrating. One morning I touched the bed and swore, in the haziness of sleep, that it was indeed vibrating from the movement of my body. I've since learnt that this is called an 'internal tremor', imperceptible to others. No one understands the exact mechanisms that create this sensation, but I will likely experience them for the rest of my life. These tremors have become my canary in the coalmine, ramping up at times of stress or exhaustion. When I am suffering, I am quite literally shaken to my core.

While I am recovering, recovery, in so many ways, has begun to feel like a journey that has no end. The fact that an event takes place at one particular point in time doesn't mean it stays there. It happens over and over, ricocheting erratically through parts of your life you can't anticipate. Just as the events of my childhood came back to me so many years after I thought I had recovered from them, my physical trauma resurfaces time and again – usually when I think I have finally tamed it.

———

When I fell sick in Melbourne, my parents were in Europe. As it became clear just how sick I was, my mother stopped answering my phone calls. Perhaps my father too, or maybe he never knew; busy at work, I relied on her to relay the details to him.

Did secrets and denial prevent him from being 'father'? I've never asked. I just know the phone stopped being answered.

Upon their arrival back in Australia, my mother ventured down to Melbourne. When she saw me – wasted, pale, fragile and desperate – she claimed ignorance.

I had told her, 'I can't stay on the phone, it hurts too much to hold it,' and on another day, 'I seem to be losing the ability to use my hands – I can't type anymore or hold a pen.' What part of those words doesn't send alarm down the phone wire and into the heart of the person at the other end? Somehow, she didn't receive the message.

Alone, within 'family'.

———

My mother has another favourite story about me as a child that she has told my whole life.

The day I was born, the nurses offered me to her to hold.

She told them she was tired and would rather a cup of tea.

The amusing part of this story is how shocked and appalled the nurses were when she told them to take me away and let her sleep.

———

Once my mother realised my illness was a matter of life or death – or maybe when she just couldn't deny it any longer, even to herself – she leapt into action. She arranged appointments for me with specialists. She flew from Canberra to Melbourne to attend those appointments, staying in our spare room in Brunswick, in the old factory we lived in, then heading home after we'd been handed a new set of drugs.

There were so many drugs. Opioids, benzodiazepines, others from classes of drug I'd never heard of. Two stick out in my memory. One slowed my heart to an irregular forty beats a minute. I stopped taking that one after twenty-four hours. The other had the most astonishing array of side effects: a high akin to ecstasy; ringing in the ears; panic; and heart palpitations so severe when the dose was reduced that I had to ease off it over the course of weeks, it left me with a strange indifference to alcohol that lingered for years.

One day, unable to take the pain anymore, because none of those drugs ever did work, I insisted my husband take me to emergency. My mother flew down, meeting us at Epworth Hospital in Melbourne's east. By the time she got there I'd been given a bed and was waiting on MRIs and more tests. She came into that emergency department cubicle and did what mothers are supposed do – she implored the doctors to pay attention, to try to figure out what was eating away her daughter. She fought on my behalf. She fought for my life.

I weighed 43 kilograms; I'd lost every shred of muscle on my body both from being unable to move due to pain, and from the energy my body was using up in its efforts to destroy itself. I had dark circles under my eyes, eyes which my friends tell me now looked deadened and blank during that time. Chronic pain teaches you to live in a single point of light – there is no future, the past is dreamlike. There is just now.

Sometimes I see people in the chemist, and I recognise them as fellow travellers. That same tired look on their face, empty eyes coupled with a distracted confusion and boxes of tablets. That's what unrelenting pain does to you.

During that time, I had glimpses of 'mother'. When we were in the same city, she would drive me to the local pool to slowly walk lengths next to me, wave her arms and legs gently in the water with me to try to recover strength and reduce the pain.

She even listened to hard truths. Once it was clear I would recover, I told her a secret from my sickest months. I told her that I had kept every drug I'd been prescribed by every doctor. Enough drugs to kill me five times over, and probably in five different ways. I kept them in a basket under the bathroom sink.

Having that basket of drugs gave me great comfort. I'd think about it at night as I lay rigid in bed. I would sit in the bath and stare at the cupboard I kept it in. I spent a lot of time sitting in hot baths. My autonomic nervous system was stripped, leaving my sense of heat and cold off kilter. I could sit outside in the sun in 42-degree heat and not break the slightest sweat. Heat, and hot water in particular, eased the muscle spasms caused by the shredded, misfiring nerves. When I looked at the cupboard, I knew that if I couldn't continue to endure, I had a way out.

When I told her about the basket, my mother was shocked by my honesty. I spoke a hard truth, something she has never been able to do and certainly not in the year of cancer.

She has never denied or tried to cover over how close I came to death – by disease or by my own hand. When I told her that the pain was so severe I had been stockpiling drugs, she told me I was strong. She meant it. I could see the shock settle on her face; the realisation of a loss she had narrowly avoided. On some level, I think she revered my strength – my refusal to look away from horror. To stand in the truth of a given moment. Perhaps her own dying would have been less painful if she too had this ability.

CHAPTER SIX

Different sides of the same coin

Sometimes I think the vulnerability that pushed me into the path of danger as a child is the other side of the coin of the fearlessness that pulled me back.

―

When I was sixteen, I became furious about what had happened to me. What David had stolen from me. I would show up at his house – the one with the front garden – to confront him, taking my parents' car in the middle of the night even though I only had a learner's permit. I would drive from the wealthy eastern suburbs of Adelaide to his shitty rundown house in that rundown suburb on the other side of town – a different world – with the sole intent of asking: 'Why?' Why did you do this? Please, tell me why.

And we would sit on his verandah, overlooking the tired 1980s red-brick apartments across from his house, just visible through a large frangipani tree he always adored. Perched awkwardly on old, torn floral armchairs left outside to weather, though no worse than the furniture inside the house. A house I dared not enter.

There we would sit. Like old lovers who feel the need to revisit and dissect what went wrong – that dangerous kind of yearning to uncover a common truth that might set us free from our past but ultimately fails to leave us satiated.

And he would try to explain.

His answers didn't satisfy me then, and when I look back, I can see why. They were the typical answers given by predators: you didn't seem young; you were special; I loved you. *I still love you.*

We only had those conversations two, maybe three, times. Each time, I would drive across the city to sit on his verandah, avoiding his gaze – staring at that frangipani tree. One of those times, I showed up to find he had shaved his hair off. He'd always loved that long black hair, even after we all moved on from 1990s semi-grunge, semi-goth fashion. He tried to say that shaving off his hair was a symbol of how distraught he was; he did it 'for me'.

I scoffed; 'I lost my childhood and you lost your hair? Try harder, David.'

Different sides of the same coin

The hollowness of his words really struck one night years later, in my ever-shrinking room at the back of my parents' house in Canberra. As the months wore on, I amassed books on death, grief and trauma which sat in small stacks on top of the chests of drawers that lined one side of the room.

One of those books was David Harrower's one-act play *Blackbird*, about a woman who, at the age of twelve, was molested by a forty-year-old man. Una, the girl – now woman – finds him fifteen years later and confronts him. She is torn between the love her twelve-year-old self felt and the rage of her adult self.

By way of explanation, Ray, the perpetrator, says:

You surprised me
You made me laugh
[. . .]
You were lonely
Before you met me
When you met me
You were alone.
You were a lonely child.
You never said but when I held you in my arms I could
    feel it
[. . .]
You knew about love,
You knew more about love than [my girlfriend] did
Than I did.

You were sick of being treated like a child.

The last thing you wanted was to be told you were a child

Una, now an adult, retorts:

That's what children say.

Harrower's play is based on the real crimes of Toby Studebaker, who abducted a twelve-year-old British girl in 2003. Studebaker groomed his victim over the internet. The Studebaker case is credited with leading to the first Scottish laws against child grooming over the internet and, more broadly, of alerting the world to this new danger.

A friend who is a lawyer in South Australia once told me my own case, which started in early 2000 and finally ended in 2002, was the first internet-related case of stalking and harassment – grooming, if you will – in South Australia. If this is true, it's an eerie and appropriate parallel, given the similarities between the words Harrower puts in the mouth of his predator and the ones that I have heard from my own.

I don't know how Harrower managed to capture so accurately the dynamic between perpetrator and child victim without being on either side of that equation himself. Maybe these men are more transparent from the outside than you realise when you are the one trapped within their web, when you are their prey.

What strikes me most about *Blackbird* is that Harrower

Different sides of the same coin

captures Una's warring emotions. In the single scene that makes up the entirety of the play, Una insults, hits, kisses and threatens to expose Ray, and then begs him not to leave – hating him and loving him all at once. It's as though she is simultaneously twelve and the adult she has grown into.

I don't feel that inner turmoil now, but I remember a time when I did. In the process of pressing charges and taking David to court, the public prosecutor rang me one evening to tell me a hearing had been delayed because David had tried to commit suicide.

My response: 'Is he okay?'

Before I'd officially pressed charges, when I was still attempting to extract answers from David that would satisfy me, I once rang an ambulance for him. That night we had talked on the phone, not on his verandah. He had rung me one night on my mobile and, after mumbling incoherently, announced he was going to kill himself.

He said: 'I have a problem. I can't stop. I'm going to kill myself because I can't stop,' and then hung up.

Instinctively, I rang 000.

Lying in the same childhood room, the very same bed, where the events I was seeking answers to had occurred, I even called the ambulance service back an hour later to ask if he was okay.

They said he was 'known' to them, by way of explaining that he was fine.

I think when family doesn't work for you as a child and you find, or are found, by something else, 'family' gets muddled up. Even through the anger and my decision to expose David, he was somehow family to me. There have been moments in my life where I have had the urge to find him and say, Look – *look who I have become. I have a PhD, I do important work, I have loved ones, I am whole.*

Like a child to an aloof parent.

Unsatisfied with David's answers, furious with his statement that he 'couldn't stop', I pressed charges. That is no easy thing to do when a case involves sexual assault and is now nearly four years old. I didn't have the letters because I had destroyed them after stealing them from my mother's nightstand. Nor did I have any witnesses.

He pleaded guilty and the matter was settled. I never stood in front of any court; I never spoke of all the things he had done to me in front of an audience. To be honest, I do not think my courage would have extended that far.

Instead, I sat in small offices across the table from police and, later, a public prosecutor. They always put a box of tissues on the desk between us. I never needed them.

The public prosecutor remarked on my stoicism, a little surprised. But I was fuelled by rage and fear, and felt far too numb to breakdown in public. It was the numbness that had enabled me to enter that office, that building, in the first

Different sides of the same coin

place. Some things never change; I do this now when people ask me about my mother. I give them facts – straight up, no emotion. I serve it up cold.

'How is your mother doing?'

'She's dying.'

I know it isn't what people expect and that it can seem like I'm not deeply, irrevocably, affected by these intertwined tragedies – childhood abuse and a dying mother. But tears are something I do in private. My grief is private, often even from the people who love me.

While David agreed to plead guilty to many of the charges – though not all – we still played a game of tug-of-war through our lawyers. A game that, like real tug-of-war, leaves you bruised and muddy even if you win. He quibbled over minor details in my statement – a statement given at age seventeen about events that took place between the ages of twelve and fourteen.

Sitting in those offices, with their big lawyer-desks, we combed through his requests. He wanted minor amendments. Strange, funny little things – like the wording of things I claimed he had said to me, the exact order of events. Things that ultimately made no difference to his fate. Yes, the devil is in the detail, but when you're already pleading guilty to sexually molesting a child I'm not sure it matters if you said to that child: 'Why won't you have sex with me?'

While I let go of the idea of his pleading guilty to all the charges the police brought against him – recognising

I was lucky he was admitting guilt at all – I did insist on one thing. One crucial thing that no one at the time could have possibly predicted would shape the course of David's sentence and life in profound ways. Something that seemed almost arbitrary at the time.

I said I would forgo the statutory rape charges, I would forgo a public court case, if David pleaded guilty to charges across two time points – the start and the end of the abuse. I did this because I wanted the record to reflect that I had been stalked, groomed and pursued over a period of years.

It was not a one-off incident. I had been hunted.

The only time I stepped into court was on the day of David's sentencing. I didn't have to attend, but I wanted to; I wanted to see that I'd succeeded and that this would all be over, not yet understanding that some things are never truly over. Sometimes they resurface many years later because they were about so much more than you could possibly grasp at the time.

The courtroom of the South Australian Magistrates Court wasn't like the courtrooms you see on television. It was just a room in an office tower made of glass.

The room itself did not have windows. It looked almost like a stage set the way they'd put it together – a dark mahogany box for the stand and an equally dark wooden judge's bench, both placed in a large conference room with

Different sides of the same coin

rows of nondescript office chairs for lawyers and anyone witnessing the proceedings.

Sitting in one of these rows, I watched as David was called up to the stand. He came in through a door to my left, just near the oddly placed 'witness box'. His hair had grown back down to his shoulders, jet-black as always. He was wearing a pale blue shirt, undone at the collar – no tie, no jacket. Crumpled cream pants.

He looked smaller standing in that box with his guilt on full display. Smaller in matter. He didn't look like a predator anymore – the kind of adult man who takes the first kiss from a child and then mocks her for being bad at it; he looked uncomfortable, afraid and uneasy. Despite the adrenaline and my own discomfort at sitting in this room, looking at this man in this most serious of situations, he didn't frighten me that day.

He frightened me many days after that, and a great many before, but that day he didn't.

They read the charges – multiple accounts and variations of sexually abusing a minor. He pleaded guilty. And then it was over.

Standing outside the courtroom in the bright hallway, we looked at each other for the very last time. Each of us was standing with our lawyers, maybe twenty feet apart. I was dressed for a funeral – all in black, with a necklace that had belonged to my grandmother made of white glass Venetian beads that could be mistaken for tiny sea shells. He glanced over at me at the same time as I turned to look at him.

We had always met in secret. In the dark. In small hushed rooms.

It felt so strange to lock eyes with him there. In a public space, in the brightly lit corridor of a high-rise building. The intimacy of the look he gave me was undone by the surrounds. 'This isn't your game anymore, David,' I thought. The rules had changed. I had changed them. No longer a child who existed in classrooms and bedrooms. Now, dressed in black with small high heels, looking like the adult I had just become, I existed in different rooms. Rooms of power, of authority. In these spaces he was diminished, while I was emboldened – prey no more.

Through the network of police and lawyers I was told that he believed he'd pleaded guilty to save me the humiliation of a trial, to avoid putting me through more trauma. The addled words of an addled mind or a perpetrator still weaving his web; 'I love you', 'I care about you', 'I have done this thing for *you*'.

And again, Harrower's play rings true. Ray says:

> When I couldn't find you that night,
> I thought something must've happened to you.

Different sides of the same coin

[. . .]
Someone had taken you
Someone was
Harming you
Even thought maybe
Maybe I should go to the police

When [the police] found me I was on the floor of the
   phone box.
Hugging my knees.
Crying my eyes out
Because I had lost you
I hadn't protected you.

Actually, David pleaded guilty because of very good police work. They took his computer, they searched all the files, they pressured him into admitting guilt. But once again, I do not really know the full details. I never asked.

That's the last time I ever saw David, in that hallway.

It isn't the last time we ever spoke.

———

I recall at the time feeling, and saying over and over, that I didn't want him to do it again to someone else. And I didn't want him to go on to live a happy life with children, a wife and a goddamn picket fence when he had pursued, hunted and killed my childhood. Of course, now I see he wasn't the only one to kill my childhood – I didn't wander into his path a happy well-adjusted child. My disconnection from 'family' placed me in his path.

I do know, because we live in the age of the internet, that I got my wish. Between his growing mental health struggles and the strict child sex offender laws, he never went on to live any kind of life one might describe as normal. No job, no partner, and continuous monitoring by police. For all I know, he still lives in the same shitty rundown house in the same suburb in the west of Adelaide with a frangipani tree out front, less than ten kilometres from where he grew up and has spent his entire forty-five years of life. Though, as has happened in so many Australian cities, gentrification has likely pushed him out to the fringes of the city, like refuse.

I suppose that's what justice looks like, but I don't take satisfaction from this as an adult, even though I know that teenage me would have. I am pleased for teenage me; I'm pleased she got what she wanted.

What about adult me, you ask? Adult me sees the world as far less black and white.

Crimes of sexual assault against children are said to carry such heavy penalties because the victims must carry the burden for the rest of their lives. I don't know if sentencing someone to a life of poverty, paranoia and decaying mental health is justice. I don't know if I believe in justice in the colloquial sense: an eye for an eye. But maybe it is justice in the sense of the word as actually defined. The *Oxford English Dictionary* reads: 'a concern for justice, peace, and genuine respect for people'. I wanted peace for myself, and I wanted vulnerable girls to be respected – to be safe.

Regardless of any ambivalence I feel as an adult, I didn't make the child sex offender laws, or the various legal amendments that came into being throughout the 2000s, which tightened those laws considerably. Someone convicted of the crimes that David pleaded guilty to can no longer leave the state without registering with both South Australian police and the police of the state they are visiting.

What became crucial under the reforms is the number of acts and the age of the child. Forcing David to plead guilty to acts when I was twelve and then separate acts when I was fourteen – something that at the time made no difference to his suspended sentence or its conditions – became the difference between him being someone who could resume a normal life and someone who would be monitored forever by police. With the reforms to the South Australian Child Sex Offenders Act in 2006, and then again in 2007, a person found guilty of abusing a child under thirteen and for multiple incidences of abuse is placed on the Sex Offenders Register.

Making him plead guilty to incidences separated by years counted as separate offences under the new reforms.

That demand I had made years before grew teeth under the legal changes of the mid 2000s: teeth that ripped up any chance of him having a normal life.

The Australian registries aren't public as they are in some parts of America, but they are used by police to monitor the activities of offenders. People like David are subject to routine reviews. Every time police stop them, even for a minor traffic offence, there it is in black and white: REGISTERED CHILD SEX OFFENDER. These laws may soon be extended nationwide, spurred on by the rise of 'helicopter parenting' and our growing preoccupation with risk. The bizarre phenomenon of 1990s media personality Derryn Hinch finding his way into the Australian Senate in 2016 on the platform of preventing and punishing paedophilia is but one outcome of our growing anxiety over children and their safety. I don't disagree with the strengthening of these laws, but the social shift that is driving it makes me feel more conflicted.

I often think about a series of studies I once read. They were based in towns in England and America and traced how far children were allowed to roam in the 1950s, compared to now. The footprint has shrunk from kilometres to metres, despite stable crime rates and no known changes in other types of risk.

We think that making children's worlds smaller – more fearful – will keep them safe. In my experience, it can push them towards danger.

———

Because of the legal changes that have occurred, this much I know: David will never hurt another child again.

I take solace in this. But as an adult I also understand more about what intergenerational abuse does to people and about mental illness. I'm not saying I feel sorry for David, and where he ended up. I'm saying that, as a society, we haven't yet figured out how to deal with these types of crimes or the people who commit them.

What I did conveyed fearlessness and strength; I know that. Pressing charges when I was just seventeen. Taking a man who abused me as a child to court when I was still, developmentally if not legally, a child and doing it without the support of family or friends. I had just one psychologist going above and beyond, and one dedicated detective.

I spoke to that detective not long ago. Once I began excavating my past, I wanted to know what the Child Sex Offender Registration Act meant for David. I sent him an email and he rang me the next day and explained everything he could within the bounds of what he was legally permitted to tell me.

Somehow, I thought that he would remember me. Because of my fearlessness. He didn't – I'm sure he's seen too many things to remember one young girl fighting to put herself back together again through the criminal justice system. But I wanted him to remember me. Maybe I should have told him how grateful I was for what he did. I didn't. He tried to comfort me, anyway.

'Don't worry, it's not like this person is in the community without us keeping an eye on him.'

I thanked him awkwardly and hung up.

———

The few people I've told over the years about taking David to court have marvelled at my strength. The courage it took to do that. I've never been able to answer how I managed such a feat.

I wonder sometimes if it's the same fearlessness that enabled me to slip out of my house into the night with a strange man.

While the consequences may have been dire, it takes a certain amount of strength and bravery to head out into the darkness with a stranger. There is strength in reaching out for something different when 'family' doesn't work for you. And there is strength in fighting to be heard as a child over and over, even when it leads to yelling and being locked out of your home.

Sure, they're not sophisticated tools. They're the tools of a confused child. But there is strength in fighting for something beyond what you have been given.

———

So, I have a happy life for the most part – a successful life, if you will. Though success can be deceptive. Success can, in fact, be running away. It can be building a wall. Success can be accumulated out of a desperate search to feel safe.

Just like my mother and her neat boxes filled with jumbled odds and ends, everything can look perfect from the outside. Just don't open the lid.

But still, I have a successful career, friends, a dog, the markers of middle-class normality. I have these despite all that could have so easily upended it – all that could have pushed me past the point where I could take the things that have happened to me and use them to grow, even if they are hard to swallow, as writer Cheryl Strayed suggests. There is a point where you cannot become *more* than the things that have happened to you, and they devour instead of nourish you.

That's not to say that at times, especially in my youth, life wasn't messy and chaotic. Or that I didn't hurt myself and others in my efforts to disentangle myself from my trauma and exorcise my past. Through my late teens and early twenties I left behind me a wake of destruction, unable to comprehend that other people had feelings – feelings that mattered. That I could make them feel and hurt and suffer as much as I did, though in different ways.

The author Cheryl Strayed, explaining how she put herself back together after trauma, said she was sorry for the people she hurt, but not sorry for the things she needed, for what she did to heal herself. Those aren't her exact words, though the sentiment is the same, and it's a sentiment I share.

There are a great many people I'd like to say sorry to. To tell them, show them, why I was the way I was and did the things I did. That I was broken and trying to work out how to fix myself, but no one had ever given me the tools and so I had to figure it out on my own.

In time, I found my feet. I stopped hurting people. I began accepting love. I built a life. It helped that my family left Adelaide and I stayed behind and then moved to Melbourne on my own to start afresh when I was twenty-two. I found a new kind of safety.

David once asked me, during one of our confrontations, how, if I were so damaged by what he had done, could I be doing so well? How could I be as strong and together as I was?

I didn't say it at the time, but I've said it over and over to myself since: my successes and my strengths were despite him, to spite him. They were not because of him. And they absolutely are not to be twisted and contorted into strange excuses for his actions, or taken as an indication that I was not *really* harmed by what he did.

But I have to wonder how many parts of my life, of my 'success', have his fingerprints on them. Is my relentless pursuit of perfection – the career, the home, the marriage, the dog – an attempt to prove I have outrun him? Success can be a life well lived. But it can also be used to hide from things we do not wish to confront. Like fearlessness, it can be a coin with two sides.

CHAPTER SEVEN

Hail Marys

I've told you I have a sister. But I haven't explained to you yet how she fits into this story.

While I looked for safety in dangerous places, my sister looked for it in books. Hanging on my parents' wall there is a photo of her and me as children. We have made a swing on a Hills hoist out of an old hose. Dangling from the metal strut opposite that holding the swing is a single line of hose – a handle. In the photo, I am sitting on the swing and my sister is pulling me around in circles using the handle, her head buried in a book. That photo encapsulates our childhood relationship for me. Me demanding the world pay attention, her disappearing into books.

She has her own story about 'family', about being alone in 'family', and it's not mine to tell. But I will sketch you an outline of what I know, what I see of that story from the outside.

I asked her, while writing this book, if she felt alone as a child. She said yes. How could it be that we were both so alone, and yet right there next to each other? Why couldn't we reach out and hold each other up, embody that thing that we were – 'sisters'?

She speculates that it is because our mother was such a destructive whirlwind – through our household and through our lives – that every other interpersonal relationship got swept up with it. Flying through the air in circles around my mother and her infinite matter, we couldn't see or reach each other.

We hid from her, and as a result each other. She with her books. Me sitting on the roof of our two-storey house, where no one else dared go.

A close friend from childhood has always found it funny that when my sister was young, she thought someone was writing a book about her. Our friend's amusement has kept that story alive.

I never really reflected very much on the meaning of that story. As I said, my sister was – is – gifted in so many ways. She spoke and read at a ridiculously young age, she was precocious, she devoured books well beyond what would be considered age appropriate. Why wouldn't that intelligence also come with some quirks?

But once my mother began dying, more space has been made for us to understand one another. To begin to fumble our way awkwardly through this thing we are – 'sisters'. She told me that it has always made her angry that our childhood friend brings up that story. And one day, when reading something on psychology, she realised that it was a sign of a child dissociating. Placing herself outside herself, because being inside was unsafe.

She coped in different ways from me, and she no doubt bears different scars. But now I see there are similarities. We have shared experiences and shared pain of loneliness, of abandonment within 'family'.

―――

'Mum has always been good with small children,' my sister said on one of the many occasions we discussed our parents' pathology during her visits back to Australia in the year of cancer. 'Very small children – babies and toddlers. After you were older she didn't know how to cope.' My sister is four years older than me and remembers things I do not. She remembers my mother being good with me as a baby. She remembers it starting to fall apart when I was eight. I feel vindicated when she tells me this. It wasn't that I was difficult; I hadn't imagined the disconnection that grew as I grew, and it wasn't my fault. As we begin to feel out these new roles of 'sisters', I feel more validated in my interpretations of the past.

I have not invented this. I did not invent her.

My sister and I haven't lived in the same city since I was a teenager. She moved to Canberra soon after my parents, I stayed behind in Adelaide, moving into an apartment I inherited when my grandfather died. I then moved to Melbourne. She moved to Germany, then England. I moved to Canberra. She moved to America.

When we are in the same city, we talk. Increasingly, we talk about our parents. But when we are apart we barely interact. We are in so many ways the opposite of one another. We joke that we split the genetic pool right down the middle – chose to share nothing but a sense of humour. The chasm between our looks, our talents, is so large we cannot even feel jealous of one another. Just awe.

When my father's mother died, my sister was living in Germany. She couldn't come home for the funeral, and to be honest we just weren't that close to my father's family anyhow.

At the funeral, held in a small room attached to the crematorium, we sat through slide shows, a few short speeches. 'She made good cookies,' said one cousin. 'She helped me when I had my first period,' offered another.

I read a poem, having nothing material to say about the woman.

My sister sent a recording of herself singing a composition based on the sonnet 'Death Be Not Proud' by John Donne:

Death be not proud, though some have called thee
Mighty and dreadful, for, thou art not so
[. . .]
One short sleep past, we wake eternally,
And death shall be no more; death, though shalt die.

Hearing that sonnet ring out across the church in her perfect soprano made people gasp. Several cried.

Me? I just smiled. Proud that what she brought to that day, without even being in the room, humbled them all.

She's never said it to me, that's not her way, but I gather my sense of awe that day has been reciprocated. Once, talking to a friend and colleague of hers, I said, offhandedly, 'It's hard to be her sister.' He laughed. 'Don't think she doesn't feel the same way about you, Gem.'

I don't know if she doesn't answer my emails and texts because she is busy, or because she is so accustomed to being isolated from and within 'family'. I'm not sure if she's figured out how to be anything but alone. She's had relationships, but they're always with men who are in, or end up in, other cities or countries. She's thirty-seven and she's never lived with a partner or had a pet. I want these things for her, but it's not my path to walk and I have only just begun to truly pull myself to safety. She will have to pull herself, though I'll be waiting if she ever does.

She has a theory that my parents were never meant to be together. They met at eighteen and married when they were twenty-one, so my mother could follow my father to Oxford while he did his PhD.

She hypothesises that, in their youth, it was an exciting mismatch of personalities. Our mother: a whirlwind of chatter and chaos. Our father: an introverted maths genius from a very poor background. We can imagine him finding her extroversion exciting and her finding his intellect alluring.

My mother has always measured people's worth by the yardstick of intelligence. It has to do with her own insecurities; she was the first in her family to go to university, clearly bright, but somehow her potential was not realised in quite the way she wanted. Then, through my father, she surrounded herself with not just academics but mathematicians and physicists – the most abstract of the academic disciplines. An excellent way to layer inferiority on an inferiority complex.

I know she felt out of place at the High Tables of Oxford and the quiet parties of professors in their impressive homes with towering bookcases. I don't know how much it has changed since then, but today Oxford is still otherworldly – a sea of sandstone and spires rising out of the green of perfectly manicured lawns. Lawns with little signs: KEEP OFF THE GRASS. FOR SCHOLARS ONLY. The British author Natasha Pulley said in *The Watchmaker of Filigree Street*, 'Everybody, professors and students and Proctors the same, knew that if the sign said "do not walk on the grass", one hopped. Anybody who didn't had failed to understand what Oxford was.'

And here they were, two working-class Australians. It bothered my mother that even the butlers looked down on them, she used to tell me; being Australian in England in the 1970s placed them lower in the social hierarchy than 'the help'. These were points of amusement to my father; but when you've risen from a childhood in women's refuges to the lofty heights of Oxbridge on nothing but pure talent, social hierarchy probably doesn't concern you very much. He hasn't anything to prove.

To this day, at academic dinner parties and gatherings he sits back, relaxed, self-assured. Heckling occasionally from the sidelines with an air of confidence. He is most alive in these moments.

We have spent countless hours at the dinner table of our closest family friends, one of whom is a fellow mathematician. My father sits at the great long wooden table of their dining room, just like those long wooden tables of Formal Hall at Oxford, wineglass in hand, casually making esoteric comments to rile his friend – the world's most famous fractal geometrist, and a highly eccentric Englishman.

'I've had an excellent day!' declares Michael – always seeking to be the centre of attention. 'I drafted a theorem!'

'Aren't your theorems always drafts?' says my father with a cheeky smirk on his face.

After Michael was hosted as a special guest across India, my father spent the next year referring to his friend as 'a minor god' at various dinner parties.

My mother, following in my father's wake to England, felt a heavier burden of expectation. She hadn't earnt her place in this new world, like he had. That sense of being an imposter haunted her all her life. It followed her from Oxford back to Australia, and imbued itself in every social interaction and act of parenting that came after.

Social status has always concerned my mother. Not money, but other markers of capital: knowledge of literature, art and music. Her childhood best friend told me that she had always been that way. 'Your mother was always worried about how she seemed to others. She always wanted to marry someone who was cultured.' So while my father might have been poor in economic capital in his youth, he was fittingly rich in intellectual capital.

I know that while those places – the halls of the academy and the dinner parties of scholars – made her uncomfortable in her early twenties, she was also enamoured of them. She followed my father and his mathematics around for more than forty years of marriage, leaving aside many of her own ambitions to do so. It must make her happy, then, that my sister and I are, and always were, completely at home in those places. It's what we know best. Even now, when she is so sick, I see her sparkle with pride when I tell her about the private dinners I've attended when travelling overseas to other universities, the giving of public lectures. My inclusion in the international circle of hospitality that is the world of academia.

That same yardstick was always used to measure my sister and me. Obviously I fell short because of my dyslexia. But even my sister did too sometimes – the bar was set higher for her. When she did poorly at school she was chastised for not putting any energy into her work, with my parents knowing that she could top the class if she wanted to.

Even now I think that yardstick looms large for both of us, though in different ways. Me: the child who exceeded expectations and who is reminded of that fact regularly. My sister: doing interesting, creative and amazing work but not climbing the right academic hierarchies.

That was all reversed just before the year of cancer began, when my sister got a position at Harvard designing tiny self-organising robots. Once she'd redeemed herself, I reflected on a conversation I had had with my mother several years before, when my sister was doing a post-doc in Germany (and speaking fluent German while she did it). Neither of us was ever enough for our mother, at any age, irrespective of our successes or our abilities. 'Your sister has been under-achieving for years,' she said. Brilliance, I imagine, comes with its own weight.

When I was a child, my mother fretted that I wasn't measuring up correctly against that yardstick. She has idly mentioned over the years that my grandmother would say when we visited her in Sydney, 'Just you wait, this one is whip-smart.' I dedicated my first academic book to my grandmother for that.

My mother found it touching, not realising that implicit in this dedication was the fact that my grandmother believed in me in ways my mother had not.

My sister tells me now that I was always my grandmother's favourite. That we were alike: uncompromising and unflinching in the face of reality. And sometimes, when required, fierce. My mother says my grandmother always understood me. She died when I was young, so I have no clear recollections of how this played out, beyond enjoying one another's company, but my sister tells me that when my mother fought with me, my grandmother would protect me.

A lifelong friend said to me, in the year of my mother's cancer, 'You always were an island in your family.' Likewise, my grandmother was ill-fitted in her family of nine children, sent away to live on a relative's farm, where she gained a reputation for taming unruly horses and riding them with an impressive fearlessness.

Her siblings always found her snobbish. Perfectly poised, perfectly polished. Never a hair out of place, never anything other than the perfect outfit – even when she was doing the gardening. There's a photo of her and my grandfather in their early thirties. She is wearing a beautiful tailored suit – a skirt and jacket, right on trend for that 1940s and early 50s post-war sensibility. Her hair set in large curls that rest on her shoulders, flowing out from under a matching hat; a hat sitting at *just* the right angle – tilted ever so slightly. She looks like a movie star. My grandfather looks like a man who can't believe his luck.

At a glance there is incongruity here. A woman so elegant, and yet she would tame wild horses that no one else could ride. Horses likely to throw her to the ground – putting that poise and elegance at risk. Yet, in her, these things belonged together. These are inconsistencies we share. I too am known for my poise and grace. I'm also known for throwing off my shoes and climbing a tree – just to prove I can. Stripping off an expensive outfit and jumping into a river or the ocean at night, danger be damned.

My grandmother studied nursing in the 1950s, when women were expected to get married rather than pursue a career. When she did finally marry, at twenty-eight, it was to a man five years her junior. The people of her small rural home town criticised her for ruining his life, warning that her old age meant she was most likely barren.

One might have said she was wild, for her time.

When she died and my sister and mother and I sat around a table on the balcony of our Adelaide home telling stories about her, I said, 'Wasn't it funny how she would sneak in after dark and say Hail Marys over our beds?'

My mother and sister looked at me blankly.

'She didn't do that to you?'

'No!' they said together, laughing.

I don't know if it was a sign that she understood I was a child alone, or a child who might find her way into trouble because of that loneliness. But the fact she never felt the need to do this with my sister shows the independence my sister has radiated her whole life. She may also have been a child alone, but she didn't appear to want it any other way.

CHAPTER EIGHT

A surface with one continuous side

David had an internet alias he sometimes used – 'Mobius'.

For those who didn't grow up with mathematicians for fathers, the *Oxford English Dictionary* describes a Möbius strip as: 'A surface with one continuous side formed by joining the ends of a rectangle after twisting one end through 180 degrees.' The German mathematician August Ferdinand Möbius discovered this phenomenon in the 1800s.

A Möbius strip has a range of curious properties; for example, it is a surface whereby the inside and the outside are the same thing. Crucially, a Möbius strip has no end and no beginning. It looks a little bit like an infinity sign, though the two are not related.

Parts of this story also curiously defy the idea that all things have a beginning and an end. That all things have distinct sides.

When my husband and I accepted my mother's invitation to move into my parents' house, in the course of the endless shuffling – the assemblage and re-assemblage – many of our belongings became mixed up with theirs. I suspect we'll be unearthing things for years to come.

One afternoon, when looking for a box of personal files, I found a small box I hadn't seen before amid those belonging to me and my husband. This box was old and had a floral pattern on top against a blue background. Two ancient pieces of sellotape crisscrossed at the front but no longer held it together.

I sat down in the small available space on the floor and lifted the lid.

Inside the box was a collection of folded, yellowing papers. I picked one up, opened it; it was a letter from my father to my mother from when they were much, much younger. Before children and more life than can be counted in years. Before cancer and illness and hardship and dying.

There were periods of time my parents lived apart due to my father's work and study. This was a box of letters from those times. A whole box of love letters from my father to my mother.

I didn't read them, apart from a cursory glance at the one I picked up. The idea of my parents young and in love was too heartbreaking. I closed the box and quietly crept up to their bedroom and placed it on their bed. It seemed to me that this was a good time for them to be reminded of the strength of their young love. After all the psychosis and decay of the past year, maybe this was something they should revisit.

But before I closed the lid, I picked out one small oddly folded piece of paper with spidery handwriting all over it. It looked so askew sitting there against the pile of neatly folded letters I couldn't help myself. Upon closer inspection, I realised it was a Möbius strip.

In 1971, my father had made a love letter in the form of a Möbius strip and sent it to my mother.

> Dear Cris,
> Just a typological demonstration that a Möbius strip has exactly one surface.
> It occurs to me that women should always write on a Möbius strip as it would save them from the necessity of saying everything over and over again. Or for people who carry on circular arguments?
>
> And finally:
>
> This leaves me with just enough room to say again that I love you, and that I make the promise that I'll never leave you.

As I hold this odd little coil of paper in my hands I ache: my father loving my mother enough to make this strange little gift and posting it to her, at the age of twenty-one.

My father's words hinting that my mother was always a woman of circular arguments – illogical from the start. That we are all still caught in this same loop from 1971, or earlier. And, more importantly, I had not created it by being a difficult child.

That my father had *chosen* to be in this loop, not fallen into it, as I had always thought.

My father being a sexist idiot about women; he's come a long way since having two daughters.

But mostly: that this man sat at the tender age of twenty-one, making this gift, which he perceived to be a mathematical delight, for his lover. That he could not possibly know that one day he would have a daughter. A daughter who, for her whole life, would be filled with terror by the word 'Möbius'.

I am reminded that maybe this story did not begin with David. Maybe it did not even begin with my birth.

———

David used to say that he had a difficult and abusive childhood. His former girlfriend told me that he was in his teens when his mother kicked him out – she handed a suitcase of his things to his girlfriend's mother and basically just walked away. He never spoke much of his father.

A surface with one continuous side

Intergenerational trauma such as this is certainly socialised. It shapes our lives and minds as we grow up amid its turmoil. While the research that has attempted to reveal links between the survival of abuse and the later perpetration of abuse is mixed and unclear, David's abusive childhood has undoubtedly shaped his life in many ways. This kind of trauma also gets encoded into our very DNA. It's been shown by research into the children and grandchildren of Holocaust survivors. We carry it with us, from one generation to the next. It stretches back and forward in time, in ways we cannot always predict or understand.

I've thought about this when contemplating my mother's actions. Was there something in her past that might be like mine? There may be genetic strands that were passed down through our family lines, creating the perfect storm that was David and me.

Genetics aside, there are other curious invisible threads that stretch between David and me, keeping us in some sort of strange orbit, often without the other realising. Given I have my stories, I assume David has his.

When I was twenty and my grandfather, who lived in Sydney, died, I inherited an apartment he owned in Adelaide – an investment property of his he'd let me move into once my parents had moved to Canberra and my sister followed after them, a little later. A few years on, in my twenties, I sold that apartment so I could move to Melbourne and leave Adelaide behind.

One afternoon in 2007, the real estate agent came to the apartment to give me a rundown of how things were going with potential buyers. There were two. The first: a couple, thinking of purchasing the place for their son to go to university; it was located a short walk from the University of Adelaide, which I had also attended. The second: a man. The real estate agent didn't put much stock in this second buyer – he said he was strange. Then he said the man's full name. It was David's name.

With a trembling voice, I asked more questions: What did this man look like? What did he *seem* like? The real estate agent must have thought I was mad.

The description matched. To this day, I am fairly certain that David stood in my apartment. Walked around it.

That apartment with the walls I'd painted myself until I had blisters across both my hands, taking them from 1970s dirty purple and green to a bright white. Did he sit on my bed? My now double bed, with its crisp white sheets? Did he run his fingers over my dresser, where a small wooden box sat – open it to find a card from my grandmother's funeral, a necklace of multi-coloured plastic beads that spelt out my name given to me by a lecturer's daughter I babysat?

Had he gazed at the photos on my fridge? Polaroids taken with a birthday gift from a friend. Me and my friend Bri, arm in arm, soaking wet at a music festival. My friends sitting in a row at a favourite local pub, all dressed in vintage clothes and starting at the camera American Gothic-style.

Had he inspected it all? Then considered buying this piece of my inheritance – this piece of my *history*? He couldn't have known before entering that it was mine. But surely he knew afterwards.

The apartment went to the family with the teenage son. But for a full two weeks I walked around in a fog, wondering if the world was real. Adelaide is small, but not that small. It's the one time I've questioned – genuinely wondered – whether I was losing my mind.

———

David and I have continued to circle around each other as the years have gone on. After all, here I am writing a book about him twenty years later. Just as I cannot trace the beginning of our story, maybe it also has no clear end.

CHAPTER NINE

The start of a letting-go

Even after I sold my grandfather's apartment in Adelaide and moved to Melbourne for close to a decade, the ground still never stopped tilting towards my mother. Distance was no obstacle. And the ground never tilted more than in the year of cancer.

Through so many betrayals, small and large, I continued to fight for her. I read every piece of research. Spent hours combing information on specific drugs, dosages, side effects and prognoses. I spoke to every expert, exploiting my connections at the university where I worked, dressing up my title of 'Doctor' to provide me with legitimacy within the medical community, though I'm a Doctor of Social Sciences.

When it became obvious that death wasn't too far off, I began fighting for a good death. No more chemo, no more psychosis. No more poisoning a dying woman.

All the while, the assisted dying debate of 2016 raged in the background – spread across newspapers and TV screens, but never mentioned in my parents' house.

My mother talked about liver transplants and experimental drugs. I talked about quality of life.

Here we were at the end – her so essentially her, and me so essentially me. Offering up hands full of reality to a woman in denial.

Eventually, my help was rejected.

She didn't want the truth.

―

Before major appointments with her oncologist or palliative care team we would create a game plan together at the dining room table. I'd draw up charts, make lists of pros-and-cons of different treatments. I would tell her what I would do if it were my body shot through with cancer, then let her make her decision.

Have you ever been to a breast cancer clinic? Breast cancer is not the most common form of cancer in Australia, but it is the best funded. It's palpably obvious from the moment you enter the clinics. You shift from the standard shabby halls of a public hospital to a veritable oasis. The furniture is new, like the paint on the walls. In the waiting areas chairs are clustered together like in a cafe, not arranged in lines like your standard medical facility. And the chairs are comfortable. Some of them are recliners. You can help yourself to

The start of a letting-go

food and drink. There are nurses practically jumping out of the walls to help you. 'Don't worry,' those rooms say, 'we've got you. We know what we're doing.'

Despite the relative glamour of the facilities, I watched grey-faced women shuffle in and out of these waiting rooms like zombies – dosed up, or overdosed, on chemotherapy and other drugs – aided by family members or a walking frame. 'No,' I thought, 'this is not how we should die. This is not how I want my mother to die.' Not just because of the empty expressions and painful slow shuffling of these women, but also because of the ways in which the treatment rendered them passive recipients of the medical system. Compliant, docile creatures teetering on the edge of life and death. It takes great fortitude to say 'enough' to an oncologist, I have learnt. To walk away from the reassurance those rooms offer.

In the appointments, I would position myself in the patient's chair, even when the doctors objected – and they always did. The patient must sit in the patient's chair so they can direct their own treatment.

From the patient's chair, I advocated for my mother. I threw numbers at them, scientific papers, everything I could to force the best treatment plan. The plan that would help hold the cancer at bay but wouldn't induce more suffering. The plan she had chosen. Despite my wish that this would all be over, I sparred with those doctors, determined that she would not have a bad death. That she would not become the women I saw in the waiting rooms, with their empty eyes, walking aids and ghostly white skin. This is not living, and this should not be what we do to the dying.

In the last appointment with my mother's oncologist that I agreed to attend, my mother cut me off mid-battle to say, 'Let's listen to the doctor.' Her tone was patronising: *Be quiet, little girl, let the doctor speak now.* I knew what the doctor would say, was saying. We all did. She was saying, 'Keep doing the chemo.' Never mind the psychosis, the sickness, the complete loss of self, the destruction of everyone around you along with the cancer cells.

But in cutting me off, our game plan to get the treatment protocol she wanted unravelled. I saw it in the doctor's expression. I wasn't a daughter advocating for her mother. I was a daughter taking control away from her dying mother. It was as though I was acting on my unspeakable truth of wanting my mother's illness, her dying, to end. It's true, I wanted her suffering – or my suffering, which was interminably bound to her suffering – to end. But I also knew, as we all knew, that the chemo was killing her more brutally than the cancer.

A few days later, back home, my mother scolded me for upsetting the doctors. For getting them offside with my facts and more up-to-date reading of the literature. 'You're intimidating them,' she said, sad, and angry. Here I am, fighting for her life, trying to get the doctors to follow best international protocols, and she knows this – she knows I am a researcher with a PhD – but in this family I am still just a high-maintenance, annoying little girl.

Living with my mother means living without any linearity – it's like staggering around a maze, which moves and folds and slides beneath your feet until you have no choice but to lie down and admit defeat.

This time, I didn't fight back – but nor did I lie down in defeat and accept her interpretation of events, however skewed. I didn't want to spend another moment in that maze.

So I didn't contradict her. Not in the doctor's office, and not afterwards when she told me I was ruining her relationship with her clinician. It was the start of a letting-go. Of backing away from that maze, where I could never reach the prize of her love at the centre or find my way out the other side.

———

To be fair to my mother, she would intermittently tell me I was amazing: the way I was able to unearth the right pieces of research evidence; the way I battled on her behalf. And in her face I could see that she meant it. But rarely would this be conveyed in action, or become a constant – a new slot in our family structure that I could occupy. My father told me that no sooner had I sacrificed myself for her, won a battle, extended her life for a few months longer by demanding a particular test or finding a treatment that wasn't offered to her, she would forget. Even in her final weeks as she thanked people and hugged them goodbye, somehow she managed to forget me. I didn't get a hug. A kiss. An 'I love you'.

Over much of the course of that year, she would forget how to be anything but angry. Angry, perhaps, that we would keep living and she would not.

My grandmother, the only one I ever knew, died of cancer too, though hers set in when she was decades older than my mother – in her eighties. When she became ill she took charge of her treatment and the doctors, allowing them to resect a stomach tumour but refusing other interventions like chemotherapy.

The day she died, she walked out of her house and got into the car with my mother and grandfather. When they arrived at the hospital she kissed my grandfather on the cheek and said simply, 'This is it.'

In the year of cancer I thought of my grandmother often. Not just because of the way she would protect me as a child – for example, telling my parents they had to step in when my sister hit me. I thought of her because my mother did not inherit her grace in life, nor in the face of its inevitable end.

I wish she had.

———

My mother's first oncologist failed to diagnose her brain tumour even though she had lost all proprioception in her left leg. One afternoon, just weeks after finding the tumours in her breasts, she shut the car door on her leg as she was getting into the front seat. Slammed it shut without a second's thought, until the pain hit.

Around this time she began to stop suddenly while walking, reach out a hand to you, desperately. She was afraid she would fall over – all of a sudden it would be as though her left leg did not exist. For all intents and purposes, it was like asking an amputee to walk across the room unaided.

When the oncologist dismissed this, I told my mother we were firing him, and I would find her a better oncologist.

This new oncologist agreed something was seriously wrong. She found the brain tumour, and through further research we – my father, sister and I – found a new treatment that could kill it without surgery. And it worked.

That we'd saved her life never seemed to translate into my mother's actions, or her treatment of me. Where I would show unrelenting love and gratitude, she appeared to forget it had ever happened, continuing on as she had before.

———

Around this time, my sister visited from Boston, running the gauntlet of Trump's various travel bans, which had created worldwide chaos in the first weeks of his presidency. She came back to provide me with some respite during that year of cancer.

The four of us went to the fortnightly hospice meetings. Canberra has only one hospice, a small house overlooking the famous man-made lake that sits at the centre of the city.

That afternoon there was an alpaca visiting – Hercules. We spoke to its owner, while patting its white fur. He said he brought Hercules to visit every fortnight. 'Good,' Mum said. 'The dog can visit me.'

Once inside the nurse's room, on this particular afternoon, my sister and I asked to speak to the nurse alone, to convey our desire for 'a good death'. To explain that our mother's symptoms were worse than she would admit, that her denial meant she couldn't make decisions about how her life would – or should – end.

During our discussion, the nurse told us, as an aside, that my mother wasn't worried about her health and what the treatments were doing to her. She was worried about me. 'She can't stop talking about how you have been so sick, how this is making you sick again,' said the nurse. 'It's touching.'

My sister and I interpreted this as an evasive tactic. A way to avoid talking about her own prognosis with the nurses and doctors. To keep her denial intact.

Later, my sister discovered that my mother said to the nurse that I shouldn't be listened to. That my ideas about a good death, about pain and suffering, were tainted by my own experiences. My sister told me this as we drove from Canberra to our sanctuary down the South Coast to swim in the ocean.

I keep my eyes steady on the road in front, refusing to lose control – to let my hurt show through.

Even then. Even after all the researching, the caring, the giving of myself to the management of her dying, my physical weakness was used to cut down my emotional strength. Used to undermine my acts of compassion.

And I began to wonder, 'Is she betraying me or am I betraying myself?' Giving myself away to her in pieces that I should have known by now would not be accepted. Pieces I needed to keep for myself.

That was the day I stopped delivering her bad news. I stopped being the one to tell her she was dying. I no longer participated in my father's spontaneous, often random, calls to action: 'We must speak to this person.' 'We must look into this treatment.'

'We must what?' I began replying when my dad would pace around the living room when my mother was out of earshot. 'She's dying. There comes a point when there is nothing you or anyone else can do but let a person die. But if you "must", you can do it without me.'

That was when I finally began to withdraw from the circus of my mother's life, and the even greater circus of her death. Why this betrayal and not the others, I cannot say. But something about her using my own strength against me in this particular way finally tore down the charade of 'mother'. I didn't disappear completely. I still watched it all unfold. But I no longer gave pieces of myself away to her.

On our last trip to the ocean – that spot nestled between the bush and the sea we have always come to – I watched as organ failure begin to show.

I watched and I said nothing.

I didn't insist she return to Canberra or go to the hospital. I let her tell herself and the rest of us it was just a virus, nothing to do with the cancer. A mere coincidence. And while I watched her carefully when we were alone, one ear tuned to the sound of her asthmatic and laboured breathing, I made no call to action. I would not try to save this woman's life again, for her or my father, when the asking price was my own.

Stepping away from the circus, I slowly began uncoiling, unfolding from myself and reaching out to the people around me. The people who had been waiting there patiently with their hands outstretched for when I needed them.

My real family.

For a time, this new state of mind presented me with a conundrum. If I was no longer concerned with upsetting my mother – because I was no longer trying to force myself to see her as 'a mother' – how did that change what I should ask of her before she died? If I no longer feared upsetting her or causing an unravelling, did I want – did I *need* – to ask her about the letters? About it all? Or could I heal from the inside out? Could I watch her die and let those secrets be buried, quite literally, forever?

But soon, with a little distance, hiding out in my room, I could see things that had been more opaque before. I could

The start of a letting-go

see there must be more to my mother's life than I knew; perhaps she had her own pain. My psychologist told me that when parents are aware of their children being abused but don't act, it is usually because they have suffered similar abuse. Had something happened to my mother? To take action might mean forcing her to face something from her past, trigger an unravelling.

Meeting pain with pain rarely leaves us satisfied, I have learnt over time.

CHAPTER TEN

Whatever comes

As the year of cancer progressed, once the shock begun to recede, my father became more himself. He became more honest. Despite his silence in the face of my mother's rage and psychosis, when we were alone he ceased defending her. Those couches in the living room became our little confessional, where I would say I couldn't go on and he would talk of her meanness, of her denial, of how hard it was to be around her. And all the while he made it clear: *Whatever comes, we do not leave this woman.*

This covenant – not to leave my mother – does it apply to me too?

—

He stayed for more than forty years. This is the deal he made with himself and the promise he made to her: *I'll never leave you.* I struggled not to be bound by this contract, to convince myself that, unlike him, I *can* leave this woman. I can leave before she dies. I do not need her love.

But I cannot leave this man, this thing called 'family', completely.

My father has not had an easy life. His own father ran out on the family when he was ten, leaving my father to assume the role of parent to his two younger siblings. They were poor, and life was hard. He grew up in women's shelters in the industrial areas of Homebush in Sydney. He broke free using the only tool he had – his intellect. But even at university, when he met my mother, he was sending money to his mother for the younger siblings and still wearing his old blue high school shirts.

Because I know this story, I can understand the pact he has made: not to leave this woman the way his father left his mother. Knowing his story makes it easier to understand him and, at times, forgive his shortcomings. I know where those absences come from; I know what they are protecting.

It's different with my mother. I do not know her story. My father said, when we spoke about how difficult she was becoming one afternoon on the confessional couches, 'You have to remember she has a lot of baggage.'

'What baggage?' I asked.

'Oh, her mother got like this. Highly strung.'

I argued: 'But her mother was never cruel.'

'No.'

And the conversation was over, begging more questions than it answered.

Mothers and daughters can be hard on one another. But I don't know what made our relationship so hard, why she did what she did with those letters. And this makes it much harder to have empathy. Her past is a black box.

———

As I stepped back, my father stepped forward. When I sparred with the oncologists he sat 'like a wet noodle of a man,' as I described it to his doctor when she asked after him: sitting in the corner, tall, thin and limp. Out of grief, out of fear, out of terror and sadness. Out of a sheer inability to cope with something so hard. Whatever their marriage has been, it has been a long one, and he faces both loss and, potentially, a new beginning as it draws to a close.

My father, the mathematician, has spent my whole life travelling. When I was sick I asked my parents not to go away again. It scared me that they had been on the other side of the world when it happened and that they did not answer the phone. My father managed to keep that promise for a short amount of time. But soon, he was off again.

It was interesting to see him grounded, unable to run away and take breaks from my mother. He continued organising trips then calling them off either of his own accord or because I – with my relentless need to look denial in the face and yell truth at it – told him he could not go.

This is the one time he can't escape.

My sister thinks he feels guilty for all the time he has spent away from my mother – the time he *needed* to spend away from her. Despite the promise he made on the Möbius strip – 'I will never leave you' – he left often.

———

Watching me with the doctors gave my father more confidence to engage, to push for what my mother wanted or needed. Sometimes it still seemed like he was dashing around widely in his mind, thinking about the next action he could take. The next drug, the next intervention – the 'we musts', as I called them. Some of this might have been driven by grief and desperation. But I know, and my sister knows, that some of it was driven by guilt.

She is not an easy woman to live with. Before the cancer or after.

One Saturday afternoon, sitting across from one another in the living room, he said that my mother was lucky to have anyone left around her. She had become so mean. 'But family stick together,' he continued. A lucky woman, getting better than she was ever able to give. He went further, admitting he had found her rude and difficult for fifteen years – the exact amount of time I'd been living in another state. I guess her unhappiness needed to find a new home once I was unavailable to soak it up, so it settled upon my father.

In a quiet moment, if he was unwaveringly honest with himself, he would speak his own unspeakable truth: in this death lies both sadness and relief.

In the last weeks of my mother's life I stepped back into her dying. I looked around and saw no one else standing. And so I became control central – a one-woman command centre. It was an act of love, but one for myself as much as for her, to conduct the orchestra of her death into as smooth a symphony as I could manage. And that, perhaps, is the difference between this act and all the organising, fighting and wrestling that I had done on her behalf until that point. This act was to diminish our shared suffering.

Finally, her liver had begun to fail. She was accumulating fluid in her abdomen – blowing up like a balloon. By now she'd stopped the chemo and emerged from its delirium. Fully conscious, she watched her body expand with the telltale signs of internal decay.

At first we drained the fluid. I sat on the end of her hospital bed, back in the shabby part of the public hospital, and chatted to her idly. Occasionally I'd pick up the five-litre bag that was filling with an opaque yellow fluid and congratulate her. 'Well done! Look at all of that you got rid of!' And when tissue passed: 'Oooooooh, there's a chunky bit!' She laughed and laughed, mostly I think at my tolerance for strange bodily happenings.

During the draining, the oncologist came. It was just the two of us: my mother, and me on the end of the bed with the five litres of fluid. He told her she had only weeks to live.

She turned to me, all traces of laughter gone. 'Will you all be okay? Do we have to talk about my funeral?'

'I've got this,' I replied.

She nodded calmly. After a year of denial, it evaporated off her skin in mere seconds. I could almost see it go.

'I've done my job,' she said. 'You're all going to be okay. I've watched how you've worked together as a family. I did my job. You're okay.'

There was no part of me that could look at this woman, who had just been given her final death sentence, and speak truth to her or ask her to reveal why she had kept the letters secret.

'Yes,' I said. 'You've done your job.'

Once we returned home the palliative care team came to visit. The lead nurse, my father, mother and I sat around the dining room table and the nurse explained the medical equipment they'd be bringing in, the hospital bed they would set up. None of us said anything. None of us knew what to say.

After she left, I realised we'd allowed something terrible to happen. This wasn't the plan – she was meant to go to the hospice. She didn't want to be at home at the end. And we didn't want the house turned into a medical facility.

Once my mother returned to her bedroom to rest, I grabbed my father urgently across the table: 'No! No, this isn't what's meant to happen.'

I rang the head nurse, who tried to assure me that my mother had months left to live and, anyhow, the hospice was full. 'I know my mother,' I replied. 'Trust me, she doesn't have months to live. Things are moving fast.'

The nurse didn't believe me, and that night I spent hours on the phone organising a backup plan. I found a private hospital with a small palliative care team that would take her should things take a turn for the worse.

That whole week, since the draining, I'd made sure she was never alone. An army of friends was clocking in and out when I couldn't be there.

One afternoon my mobile rang at work. It was my friend Melissa. Something had changed she said, just in the last hour. 'She's not talking, she looks different.' She sounded worried.

After rushing home, I found my mother lying across the bed sideways. She was done up, having received guests that afternoon. A patterned navy linen dress, a red-and-grey headscarf covering her cropped hair, which had only just begun to grow back. And, as always, her bright blue eyes, which opened when I walked into the room.

'Mum! How are you feeling?'

She was awake, but distant. 'Oh . . . okay. Tired,' she replied.

Melissa was right. Something had changed. I can't explain it, but you just instinctively knew when you looked at her, the hazy way she replied to questions, that this woman was about to die.

We rang an ambulance. Melissa waited by the front door. I returned to my mother's bedroom and lay down next to her on her bed. We looked out the window at her beautiful garden.

After a little while she turned her head to face me. 'I'm losing words,' she said groggily. 'I can't . . . I can't . . .' She held up her hand and tried to touch each of her fingers to her thumb in turn. Missing each time, if they even bent far enough to get close.

'I know,' I replied quietly. 'The ambulance is coming.'

She turned her head away again, and we lay together on the bed, on our backs, looking out at the sky.

Once the paramedics came they must have sensed it too. 'Yes,' one said calmly to me, 'she needs to go to the hospital. I'd say she has no more than a week left.' The dying, it seems, have a different quality to them. You can feel their essence seeping away.

They shuffled my mother onto a stretcher – it was painful to watch; her abdomen was so large and swollen, full of fluid again. I walked behind them as they wheeled her out of the house. I watched them take her through her front door for the very last time. Feet first.

———

When my mother finally did die, after the longest year of our lives, I was in the room.

Some part of me needed to be there at the very end. To wring every ounce of pain and loss and hope out of the final days, hours and moments of her life.

The night my mother died, I knew it would be her last. I knew it even though three palliative care nurses and doctors still, *still*, kept saying, 'No, she has weeks to live.' She had been saying to me for two days, 'Just keep me going until your sister gets here.' My sister had returned to Boston two weeks before, thinking my mother had months to live. The day my sister arrived in Canberra, I knew, would be my mother's last.

Late in the evening, Melissa drove me to the hospital; my sister and father had gone home, believing they would return the next day to spend more time with my mother. Melissa and I were both fully aware we were about to observe this woman's last moments. Compelled to be present. To bear witness. Secretly hoping, still, that something important might pass between us even in the twilight of her dying.

If you ever find a friend who will stand with you in moments like this, try to keep them close. They are a rare kind of person.

We found her flailing in the bed, in pain but with no voice left to express it.

We implored the nurses to give her drugs . . . all the drugs they could.

And they did. And she calmed.

People think death is easy, or peaceful, when you're in palliative care. When you know it is coming. But even with the drugs, my mother's death was neither peaceful nor easy.

I never realised until that night how hard it is to die, even though I know on an intellectual level that I have come close myself. In her book *The Disappearance*, Geneviève Jurgensen said of her two young daughters who perished in a car accident without her, that they 'had known how to die . . . they did the whole thing by themselves'.

Sitting with my mother, holding her cold hand and listening to her forced but utterly determined breathing, it felt like she did not know how to die.

In the end, she died when our backs were turned. When we weren't holding or touching her anymore. The nurses called out and I looked around in time to see her last gasp.

It frightened and horrified and broke me, that gasp. I cried. I cried, for everything she had given me, and everything she had not.

I cried so hard three people had to hold me. I lay on the foot of her hospital bed holding her legs, folding myself into a tiny ball, saying over and over, 'I love you.'

Through all the betrayals and all the pain, as this woman finally lost her matter, all I could do was love her. When I looked at her face for the final time, I saw she'd died with a tear on her cheek.

Afterwards, we drove to my parents' house – now my father's house – and woke all the family and friends who were there to tell them it was over. To sit among others who knew the exhaustion of the last weeks, the enormity of what had just happened. And to just be.

After a little while of sitting silently at the dining table I stood up and left. My duty as her 'daughter' finished at last.

Finally, I belonged to no one but myself.

CHAPTER ELEVEN

Writing backwards

I wrote much of this book in the final months of my mother's life.

Some people will want a book about my mother's death to be about grief. People who know more of the story will want it to be about anger. Those who are more sentimental might want it to be about forgiveness.

It is about none of these things.

It is about all of these things.

———

I realise now that I have been writing backwards – from forgiveness to un-forgiveness. That over the years I made a kind of peace with David, and with my mother, in order to carry on. But it wasn't real peace; it was a temporary truce. And it was broken open when my mother began to die, and everything drifted to the surface again.

Old wounds were reopened by new betrayals; I had never really made peace with what had happened. I had merely chosen to stop thinking about it and, in doing so, arrived at a type of unconscious and unspoken forgiveness.

I'd done this, in part, because there is such a strong cultural desire for forgiveness; we believe that forgiveness is the only way to move forward. No doubt rooted somewhere back there in Catholic faith, it has spread like a virus into so many areas of literature, various forms of spirituality, law, psychology and things that pretend to be psychology. It has become the stuff of every self-help book. *This is how we move on, this is how we let go.*

Forgiveness has come to be seen as necessary for victims to complete themselves, to become whole again. A way to reclaim self-efficacy. Forgiveness is something people would have you believe you do for yourself, to end someone's hold over you.

But sometimes, despite what we are told, forgiveness isn't something we should offer up to those who have wronged us, even after sufficient penance. It shouldn't be the end point of the stories we tell ourselves about our lives. Forgiveness isn't always what allows us to move on from spectres and monsters from our past.

No, I don't need to forgive to have a future. And I can love without forgiveness.

When a friend asked me late in my mother's dying whether I wanted to forgive her, I thought of the way that Zoë

Morrison writes about forgiveness in her novel *Music and Freedom*: forgiveness 'is the sort of idea perpetrators and their associates suggest to victims for their own purposes, after all those victims have done for them already, sponging up the hatred that was poured upon them'. Forgiveness can be an extension of oppression.

I have had to learn to un-forgive.

My mother's year of dying was, for me, a process of un-forgiving her for what she had done in life before she met her death. To cut the Möbius strip. To learn that I mattered, irrespective of the gravity of her matter.

———

I don't think un-forgiving is the same as hating or resenting; they have anger at their core. As Chloe Caldwell says in her novella *Women*, 'There's that Buddhist quote, (S)he who angers you owns you. She owned me. I allowed it.'

If I were angry it would suggest I still believe things could have happened differently. That *she* could have been different. Anger, hating . . . those emotions take energy. Energy that I don't wish to give to this. For me, learning to un-forgive has been about holding the good and the bad, but most importantly the complex, sometimes nearly impenetrable, truth of what has happened here. Of what has happened to me.

By this I mean the ways in which my story does not stand alone. It is part of a story of abuse that happened to David. Of abuse that we can assume happened to my mother.

It is an intergenerational, interfamily and thickly woven story which is part of an even wider narrative of abuse and violence against women. What has helped me most is to see my story as part of this intertwined narrative that stretches far back to before I was born. Not just because the groundwork for my life was laid in the cognitive patterns of my mother – as my father recorded in his Möbius strip in 1971 – and the events that shaped them – but also because I inhabit a society that is not gentle on women, even as we continue to fight for change. I assume this truth existed much more for my mother than it does for me, and that this must be part of what brings me to this place in which I now stand.

But if I un-forgive, and I cease to keep the secrets that were never mine to keep, then this story has the potential to end with me.

―

Some friends who read early essays from which this longer story emerged asked whether I would confront my mother. Why, as time had become finite, I didn't seek answers I deserved and the solace that might come from them.

What I came to realise is that the letters, and her silence, are no longer what matters. They mattered when I was a thirteen-year-old girl who could have been protected. But they don't matter now.

There is nothing my mother could give me in the final year of her life that would heal what has happened.

There is nothing that would have been satisfactory. Because at the heart of that searching is a longing for it all to be taken away – to make it *not so*. And that is something that could not be done, not through discussing the letters or what has happened and shouldn't have happened, or what should have been done differently. Her silence, her secrets – the very essence of her way of being in the world – were the markers of someone who cannot explain their actions. Not to herself, and certainly not to others. To ask is to search, all the while knowing you will receive nothing in return.

It was to risk being pulled back into her orbit, having finally broken free.

So I never asked about the letters or the secrets that bound us for twenty years. Maybe you're frustrated with me for that, maybe you're annoyed that there is no clear resolution, that neither you nor I will ever truly know why she did what she did, and if it had anything to do with that tear on her cheek. But I don't need her answers anymore. I know now that I am made of tomorrows, not yesterdays.

When this woman I call 'mother' died, people told me they were sorry, that it is a most awful thing to lose a mother. They mourned for me, for her. Some even mourned with me. But most of them did not know that while I have always been a daughter, in many ways I never had a mother.

I should tell you, though, that I did speak to David. At a point of crisis in my mother's dying – when we found the brain tumour – I sent him a message over social media:

> It's been twenty years since we met. Do you have anything to say to me?

At the time, I had just finished working in a research centre with the world's leading experts in restorative justice. Restorative justice is the idea that victims and offenders can heal through some form of reconciliation rather than mechanisms of the state, though I use the term 'reconciliation' loosely here. This is controversial in feminist circles because of the fight that has gone into achieving even a modicum of hard justice in cases of sexual abuse, and because reconciliation is entwined with forgiveness, which places yet another burden on the backs of victims.

No doubt influenced by the sleepless, anxious haze that followed me everywhere I went at that time, I thought maybe David and I had something more to say to one another. Not a reconciliation, not forgiveness, but just . . . more. I can't write his exact words, but our conversation went something like this:

> D: I'm sorry your mother is dying, she loves you. But she knows, she found the letters remember.
> I can't stop thinking about how much harm I have

done to you. I blame myself for so much and I regret all of it.

I haven't had a girlfriend or been intimate with anyone since the court case ended. I can't get a job, I don't have a family. I mean, who would want to marry a registered sex offender? And they upgraded it too, to 'serious registrable offender' because the laws changed. I have ANNUAL interrogations by police.

There are two things I regret:

Ever going on that bulletin board, and ever being born.

I hope you understand what happens to people after a court case like ours. I can never travel, I will probably die ten kilometres from where I was born. This isn't to guilt you – I am angry at police and justice system.

You're meant to be punished for a crime so you can learn, but if there is no end to punishment what is the point? They should bring in the death penalty for this. I've begged police to shoot me.

I can't ever call the police. I was attacked last year and the police came and arrested me. Know why? They said 'we know about your . . . past'.

I'm too afraid use my real name, to be on the internet, I don't want to be murdered or be on *Today Tonight*. Like the lawyer told me I would if I took it to trial.

In these last fifteen, sixteen years you've done what? Graduated uni, worked, had a few boyfriends probably, travelled. Want to know what I've done?
I've been in self-imposed home detention.
What else can I do?

G: I often think about if I could go back in time. I would say: 'Walk away, this will destroy you both.'

D: You are safe from me; I would STILL take a bullet for you even after all this. I never stopped caring for you.
I didn't want to put you on the stand.
I didn't want you to be asked personal shit in front of strangers.
I must go now, I'm upset. I hope you heard what you needed to.

I equivocated a great deal about whether to include this conversation. It doesn't matter what David says now. It doesn't change anything – not what happened, nor what happens from here on.

It's important to me that you understand that I don't need an apology from him. There might be an apology buried in there, but for me any contrition he may feel is swamped by self-pity. He might be sorry, but my reading of his words is that his 'sorry' is solely for himself. Perhaps that is why I decided to include the conversation; to show that it's dangerous to expect things from people who have done us great harm. Time does not always bring remorse, or the right kind of remorse, and it does not always bring change. Like my mother, people sometimes die the way they lived; the course was set long ago.

In the end, David and I agreed to never speak again. And that is the only part of our conversation I know is the truth.

PART TWO

Us

CHAPTER TWELVE

You have broken us

'You may have fucked him, but, honey, I'm his daughter,' I spat at my father's mistress.

———

It's remarkable how, just when you think you have no more heart left to break, someone finds that tiny piece that is still just, *just*, big enough to be crushed into something smaller.

I thought watching my mother die of cancer – my terribly flawed, difficult as hell, yet still loved mother – broke everything I had. Broke my heart, broke my marriage, broke me open in such fundamental ways that I became somehow different. Maybe even healed.

I was wrong.

I have learnt that there are always more parts of you that can be broken.

One afternoon in early autumn 2017, a few months after my mother died, I bump into my recently divorced husband in the driveway leading up to my father's house, where I am still living. He is there to collect some belongings he'd left behind. We are in that awkward phase of divorce when you are still talking as though you are part of each other's lives but are also beginning to realise that you are now strangers, both a little numb to the full reality of the situation. He doesn't know I'm on my way to smash every family photo in the house I can find at the end of my adulterous father's bed. At that moment, neither do I.

'In our whole marriage I never saw you ten percent as angry as you are right now,' he says, wide-eyed, as I stride past without saying a word. 'It's scary.'

My whole body radiated anger. Anger is easier than sadness. It rushes to the surface quicker than grief. Bubbles up and bursts for all to see – unlike yearning, which lingers deeper and more stealthily at our core.

Anger is about action. Grief . . . well, grief is about silence, stillness. I was not yet ready for what waited for me in the silence that was to come.

When I walked through the front door of what is now

my father's house, I was driven by an overwhelming desire to make the figurative literal.

'You have broken us, you have broken "family",' I thought to myself. The family I hoped would be built in the space left by my mother's death.

'Here, Father,' I growled as I walked through the house to his bedroom, taking photos from the walls as I went. 'Here is what you have done. To me. To all of us.'

I stood at the end of his bed – the bed where my mother and I had gazed at the sky while we waited for the ambulance. One by one, I held the photo frames above my head and released them, letting them smash in a pile on the floor.

'This is what broken looks like – it looks like smashed picture frames and torn photos of two little girls playing under a tree. It looks like ruin,' I said to the room and the ghosts of the parents I had known. 'It looks like thousands of pieces of glass that you will have to spend the rest of your life trying to glue back together. And even if you do somehow manage to, the cracks will always be visible.' Two little girls playing under a tree, overlaid by a glass mosaic with smudges of glue. They are still there, but the picture is different. Irrevocably so.

In the days before this physical smashing, I smashed my father emotionally. I told him what it was like to watch my mother die. That as her organs dissolved from cancer, black liquid began pouring from her mouth. That I watched her drowning, choking on this liquid – on and on – for hours. I smashed his solace, built on the lie of a peaceful death I had promised him she had.

I told him he had never deserved that solace.

I also sent him a story. A story about a girl who was sexually abused as a child. Whose mother knew and didn't help her. But the girl went on to grow up strong and amazing, and then nursed her mother through cancer despite such a fundamental betrayal. I told him that the story was true, that I was that little girl – smashing his idea of 'protective father'.

And with those acts, I set in motion a series of events that would lead me to the truth of my mother, whether I needed it or not.

CHAPTER THIRTEEN

We shouldn't be so disposable

In the days after my mother's death, while my father disappeared, we cleaned her sick room. We cleansed her house.

The morning after her death, sleep deprived and somewhat anaesthetised, I took all the evidence of cancer from her bedroom. A black caddy full of pills, equipment and needles. From her bathroom, more pills and the expensive make-up and adhesive eyelashes I had bought her when she started chemotherapy and was distressed by the transformation from woman to cancer patient. I dragged them all into the dining room, a mess of boxes and pills spread across the table and the floor.

We sat around the family dining table, the table of great intellectual debate, of medical discussions and decisions, and sorted through the piles – my sister, our close friend

Sammie, who is a doctor, and I – distributing the objects into three groups: useful, rubbish and a third which I called the 'could kill you pile', consisting mostly of palliative care drugs.

Next, my sister and Sammie cleaned the kitchen. They tidied the house. They began to throw out the detritus that had accumulated over the last year – over a lifetime.

Eventually my father reappeared. When he did, he didn't clean. He didn't cleanse.

He purged.

First, he went to the bedroom, taking my mother's clothes from the wardrobe, the drawers, and piling them on the floor in the middle of the room. Indiscriminately, throwing everything from old nightgowns to silk dresses into a heap, ready to be shoved into garbage bags. He took her jewellery from the nightstand, from a frame on the wall she'd had made to hang her large colourful necklaces. He put them in a box and placed it in the back of his walk-in wardrobe, where in the coming weeks it would be joined by her ashes.

'We shouldn't be so disposable,' I thought to myself, watching from the relative safety of the bed as the room was dismantled around me. But I also understood that she had to go. So much of her had to go so that we could go on. So he could go on.

How could I know what it is like to lose your partner of forty years? How could I know what you need to do to survive that great a loss? Who was I to judge how this man coped with what had just happened?

And so I let him purge. The sight of such forthright and determined erasing unsettled me and thrilled me in equal measure. 'We are starting again,' I thought. 'This year of cancer is over. We will build a new family.'

———

On my mother's birthday, several weeks after her death, I walked out of a meeting at work crying. Pushed my chair back from a meeting table with fifteen people clustered around it and walked straight out the door without a word. I was drowning on air and academic debate. I made it outside the building; my face, my hands, my sleeves wet with tears and snot.

At the funeral I did not cry.

I read the most heart-wrenching piece I could find. I brought down the house, but didn't shed a tear when I stood at the front of a large echoey church, my mother's coffin to the left of me, and read the words:

> ... there isn't one good thing that has happened ... that we haven't experienced through the lens of our grief. I'm not talking about weeping and wailing every day ... I'm

talking about what goes on inside, the words unspoken, the shaky quake at the body's core. There was no mother at our college graduations. There was no mother at our weddings. There was no mother when we sold our first books. There was no mother when our children were born. There was no mother, ever, at any turn for either one of us in our entire adult lives and there never will be.

I chose this piece, 'The Black Arc of It', from Cheryl Strayed's *Tiny Beautiful Things* – because I felt like it represented both sides of my grief: the grief for the mother I had lost, and the grief for the mother I never had. It seemed to capture the corporeal loss of my mother as well as her emotional absence throughout my life, while keeping this double meaning cryptic enough to be unoffensive.

I didn't cry at the funeral. But my mother's birthday, and its proximity to her death, completely undid me.

Late in the evening, still living in my parents' spare room, I went looking for a piece of her. I looked in every drawer that used to be hers. 'Just a t-shirt,' I thought. 'That will suffice.' But my father had thrown every last thing away.

No. We absolutely should not be so disposable. What had at first seemed understandable became a harsh slight – on her, on 'family'.

That night I needed to find something of my mother.

I needed it the way you want something when everything else has been taken from you. It became primitive.

Such moments defy logic, but much of grief does; if I could hold something of hers, put it to my face and breathe in the smell of it, the pain would diffuse. But I couldn't have this small bit of medicine; he had cast it all away.

Within a week of her death she had been all but erased.

What I didn't know at the time of the great erasing was that my father had begun careening out of control months earlier. Unravelling without anyone noticing, well before my mother's death.

I continued to live with my father after my mother died, while the house that I was meant to live in with my husband was still being built. The house I would eventually move into alone. I took frequent trips interstate, partly for work, partly just to be somewhere else. Anywhere else. While my father stayed still physically, he too was running away from the events of the last year.

One afternoon alone in my father's house in late March, little more than a month after my mother's death, I went to his study. On the wooden table that was once my grandparents' dining table sat his laptop. I wanted to look at my mother's email account, still logged in on his computer. I'd developed a new habit – I would search for my name and read emails she had written to others about how proud she was of me, how much she loved me. With her death so much anger had dissipated, leaving me with a less complicated sorrow.

As I sat at the computer, scrolling through emails, searching for a piece of my mother, a message popped up.

> I think I left an earring at your house. You better find it before anyone else does ;)

Startled, I opened the messages and read back through the texts sent between my father and a conspicuously named 'L.B.'. 'Subtle, Dad,' I thought to myself acerbically, 'one entry with initials instead of a name'.

The messages were the typical sort of messages between lovers: *Meet me here at this time. Did you enjoy the meal I made you? I look forward to seeing you again.* Sprinkled throughout were details that hinted at something more nefarious: she worked as a casual employee in a bar; she was studying mathematics at university. My father imploring her to not quit maths, just as he had done when he wrote to my mother in his twenties. Those letters sitting in the box with the lid covered in flowers. The world began to spin.

Was this one of my father's students? I wondered, horrified.

I scrolled all the way back to the start of the messages,

skipping over most of them, not wanting to know. When I reached the first message I lurched forward with shock.

I had thought my father was seeing someone. The idea didn't fill me with joy, but it also didn't upset me. My mother was gone, it was his life, he had every right to seek comfort. But this first message upended those sentiments. The message was sent the day after my mother's death from my father to L.B.

It read:

You can reach me on this number now.

———

As I later wrote in an email to my father:

You forget, I'm a millennial. I can Facebook stalk like a motherfucker.

With the few details I had, I found L.B. in ten minutes.
She was twenty-eight.
My father was sixty-eight.
She was not his student.
My father had always sneered at professors who took off with their students or assistants. Mocked them; how ridiculous it looked, how foolish everyone thought them. She may not have been his student, but in that moment a lifetime of his integrity, of my admiration, collapsed.

Sitting in my room down the back of the house, staring at L.B.'s Facebook page, pieces – suspicions I had had – began to fall into place.

The 'friends' he'd been going to jazz gigs with. When did my father ever have friends who went to jazz gigs?

The vegan lasagne in the fridge of a man who has barely eaten a vegetable in his life.

Most alarmingly, the time I came back from interstate to find different sheets on my bed. I've never known my father to change the sheets on his own bed, let alone mine.

'So that's where he draws the moral line,' I mused.

Not at an affair while his wife is dying, while his daughter sits by her deathbed. Not at having sex with someone forty years his junior. The line was drawn at having sex in his marital bed – the cancer bed. His daughter's bed? That room I'd piled my whole life into for twelve months? Well, that's just fine apparently.

Yes, he had betrayed my mother, but with her betrayal of me still etched in my skin, I thought mainly of myself in that moment. The energy I'd spent navigating her care, the trauma of watching her suffer through her last hours while he stayed away. All the while wrestling with my own past and the wretched history she and I shared.

As I wrote in a letter to my mother that she would never read, a ritual I began the week she died and continue to this day, my actions from the moment I found out about my father's betrayal were 'the only response I had. Partly for you, but mostly for me'.

When my father came home that night, I said nothing. I greeted him normally then returned to my room, where I continued to pack my belongings. Shaking with devastation, I sent an urgent message to a friend:

Can I stay at your house? Something has happened.

And I drafted that fateful email:

You've never seen how much I am your daughter.
    I'm impatient, I'm very expressive with my emotions. These make you think I'm different from you. But I am your daughter. I am so similar to you, you can't even see it.
    So I know.
    I can walk into a house and know when a woman who isn't my mother has been there. I can walk into my bedroom and know someone else has slept in my bed.
    I know she is only twenty-eight.
    I thought when Mum died the secrets and betrayal, the disrespect, would die with her and we would start again. I thought they came from her.
    And I see now that I was wrong.
    I know your secrets. Now I give you mine.

And finally:

You have a choice to make: your daughters or your mistress. You have twenty-four hours to decide; if she is part of your life, we are not.

After preparing the email I told him I was popping out for a while, quietly sneaking my bags out of the house and into the car while he tapped away on his computer in his study. Once I was done, I got in the front seat, opened my laptop, the glow of the computer screen the only light on the dark Canberra street. I attached Part One of this book to the email. I hit send.

Just for good measure, so that this great unveiling would not go unnoticed or unremarked on, I copied in the three remaining family members on my mother's side of the family whom I knew, along with several family friends. All our secrets set free at last, with the push of one button. And with that act I blew our worlds open.

I smashed them down to their foundations.

I left the rickety, rotting frame of 'family' bare for all to see.

CHAPTER FOURTEEN

Why did you do this?

In the wake of our mother's death my father had turned to face this young woman, and in doing so turned away from my sister and me. From our grief and our love. And, as if to ensure he broke things fully, beyond any kind of repair, he did it while I sat by my mother's deathbed.

What I say: 'Why did you do this?'

What I wanted to say: 'Why don't you love me enough not to do this?'

'No,' my father insisted, he had not had an affair. He *had* met this young woman before my mother had died, they had spent a great deal of time together, talking. They talked about his childhood, his life, his wife. He said her life was similar to his – growing up in women's shelters. He told me she understood things I couldn't. He could tell her things he was unable to share with us about his childhood. This only made me angrier – now my father, too, had secrets. Ones he could share with a strange young woman, someone he had just met, but not his own daughters.

I never got satisfactory answers from my father about why that young woman.

He wrote: 'I think to come to terms with the events of the previous year. I was not in a good mental state. Indeed, I was in some zombie state sleepwalking through the day and not sleeping at night. She was supportive. I do not have any idea what she found attractive in me.'

Never one to hold my tongue when I feel I have the moral high ground, I did not relent.

'I know what she found attractive in you,' I replied. 'Your money and ability to meet her unresolved daddy issues. Let me guess, she came on to you?'

My father: 'How did you know?'

This was where he went after my mother died, after the funeral: to talk with this young woman. To be with her. While his daughters cleansed the family house for him.

The two of them, my father and his mistress, seemed to genuinely believe that the fact they only began a physical relationship after my mother's death negated the emotional affair they had while she was dying. While I sat with her through her dying.

'How many days did you wait out of respect for the dead?' I yelled at my father through the computer screen. I was camped out at a friend's place by this time.

And to her, my father's mistress, 'Do you even know if her body was cold yet?'

She and I messaged each other through Facebook.

'You care only about yourself, you're selfish. What about your father's liberty of choice? You have made quite the fool of yourself.'

'Pot, kettle, black,' I fired back.

'What happened does not involve you. You are not a victim of anything. Your power trip is not warranted. You do not have the right to control anyone – no matter how it makes you feel. Maybe you can dig a little deeper and find some understanding,' lectures my father's mistress.

'Losing my father while I cared for and watched my mother die has nothing to do with me? Having to mop up the emotional distress of multiple generations of family has nothing to do with me? Having my father lie to me has nothing to do with me? People have complex lives. Actions have consequences. You are very young, but not so young you shouldn't know that. Can you really be this stupid?'

And our conversation ends. A foolish young girl for a foolish old man.

The affair is over. I don't know where either of them ever thought it would go. It went into oblivion. I sense that's all my father wanted all along – telling me he was too distressed to think about the future. For her, who knows?

I could write a diatribe about her that would take you a month to read, my fury has cooled little. But this isn't about her. Ultimately, my father's mistress – as an individual with wants, needs, desires, problems – is incidental. She was a catalyst in bringing forth the truth; evidently a useful refuge for my father; for a moment, a punching bag for me. But this isn't a story about her. It's a story about my father. About my mother.

Once we were face to face, his willingness to address the affair evaporated quickly. But I had not yet said my piece. Sitting in the living room at his house, I commanded: 'If they're too young for me to fuck, Dad, they're certainly too young for you to fuck.'
    Even at the time I could see the humour in the situation, sitting him down on the couch opposite me – the confessional couches – saying, 'No, we have to talk about this.'
    He looked at his feet awkwardly, like a child being scolded. He mumbled his agreement.

The transformation was complete – I had become my parent's parent.

———

Why did you do this?

Some friends have asked me why I was so bothered by my father's affair with a younger woman. Why I involved myself in it, demanded he end it. They thought should it happen to them, they wouldn't care; their father could sleep with whomever he pleased if their mother died.

Things are often easier in the abstract. Believe me, I would tell them, *you would care.*

The thing that these friends don't understand, that I suspect my father still does not understand, is that because he had children with this woman – my mother – he will always be her husband.

When he speaks to my sister and me, our mother is in the room. And she always will be. He can never be free of that relationship because she lives on in his daughters, irrespective of the complicated relationship we had with her. The things that she would have found unbearable, that would have crushed her with despair and betrayal, still do – through my sister and me. He may have chosen us, his daughters, in the end, but the affair will never be forgotten and it will never be forgiven either. As hard as we might try to do both those things, we cannot let go. There is some part of us that must carry the hurt for our mother, lest we betray her too.

And so it is, he can never not be accountable to his wife – dead or alive. Every decision he makes will always sit in direct relation to – will remould – his forty-year marriage.

Casting it and recasting it in a different light, making statements about what that relationship was and was not. She may be dead, but their lives are forever entwined and the memory of their marriage is not static. Even though it is over, he can still destroy it.

CHAPTER FIFTEEN
Sifting through memories

Several days after these confrontations with my father, I headed to Budapest for a work conference. By then it was April and my grief had only intensified. There began a week of email exchanges and, in time, late-night conversations with my father, as he excavated my mother's life.

Searching.

Trying to understand how this had happened right beside him, my revelations sent my father searching his memories of a forty-year marriage to a woman he thought he knew completely, but evidently did not. And he shared these revelations with me, whether I wanted to know or not.

―

I spent the days in the back of conference rooms, trying to appear normal as I chatted with my colleagues from around the world. I spent my nights in a loft in an old Budapest apartment, reading about the horrors of my mother's past, the oddities of my parents' marriage. Imploring my father to stop, just stop, torturing me with this knowledge that I didn't want. That I didn't need.

Smashing the photographs before heading to Budapest had done little to diffuse my hurt or rage. Neither did sleepless nights and work-filled days. A year's worth of pent-up pain and confusion flooded out in anger and a sadness deeper than anything I have ever known. She had died, I didn't need to be strong for her anymore. We were going to rebuild 'family', I was going to forge a new relationship with my father. Life would be different.

Life is rarely what we hope, nor is it what we expect.

Later my colleagues told me they feared for me that week. My act wasn't as convincing as I had thought.

Pale, growing thinner with every day, lost inside my own head apart from when I learnt a new horror and foggily shared it with work colleagues whom I also considered friends.

Right when I finally understood that I mattered, that I couldn't put others – my mother – before myself, with this new betrayal and the truths it led to, I became translucent.

Sifting through memories

At first, like everyone, my father was bewildered by my mother's actions. Sitting propped up on pillows in the bed of the loft apartment, bathed in blue light from my laptop at 1 am on Easter Monday, I tapped out on my computer: 'When this happens it is almost always because the parent has been abused themselves, so say all the psychologists. You're a researcher, research it: mothers who were abused are less likely to be able to protect their children from sexual abuse.'

On the other side of the world, back in his study, this sent my father down the rabbit hole. In a matter of two months he had lost his wife, discovered his daughter was sexually abused under his very roof. That his wife could have stopped it. He had damaged his relationship with his daughters beyond repair. Finally, if that were not enough, he was learning that the woman he'd married had also been sexually abused and had kept it hidden for decades.

During this time, he doesn't sleep. He alternates between ringing my sister in Boston, writing to me and attempting to ring me in Hungary. He lies awake thinking about the woman he married. Their relationship. The way it had changed over forty years. The things that had always seemed odd, that he simply 'put down to her Catholic upbringing'. And then, he puts pen to paper and pulls me down the rabbit hole after him.

How much do we ever want to know about our parents' sex lives? About their intimate relationships? As a general rule, not much. But then, as my father said, if you want the no bullshit truth, you've got to just deal with it.

My mother's life falls into two distinct parts, almost as if she were two separate people. To listen to my father speak, it is as though she woke up one day with a whole new personality. Young Cris was easy-going, gregarious, adventurous and open-minded. A little wild, you might say. Older Cris is the one described in Part One of this book – confident but difficult, combative. Living a life cloaked in denial, to the detriment of those around her.

My father tells me I never met the woman he married. The woman he fell in love with. I find this achingly sad – that there may have been a version of my mother with whom I shared a bond. Someone a little bold, a little devil-may-care. Once, in place of the mother I knew, there was a person I could have understood. Perhaps had a less antagonistic relationship with. But she disappeared and no one quite knows why.

My father blames the chronic pain that dominated her later life. Says it turned her into a 'fossil' before her time. An apt choice of word seeing that her unknown degenerative illness made it difficult for her to move, causing pain and muscle spasms throughout her body.

Maybe it was the pain. Maybe it was age. Maybe it was

something else. Trying to parent teenagers, to help them navigate the rites of those times. Perhaps it was none of these things. Perhaps it was a little bit of all of them. Regardless, I never met the woman my father married. The woman my father wrote love letters to on a Möbius strip.

My father said, in a moment of grief or truth, that he hadn't wanted to be married to her for the last fifteen years, finding her as difficult as I did. That, just as I had thought, he stayed out of obligation – illness is no justification for walking out on a marriage, on the mother of your children. How must it feel to watch the woman you love transform into someone else? I can scarcely imagine. Though difficulty can become familiar, if no less difficult.

One thing did remain constant between the two people who inhabited my mother's body – the ability to talk. Silence was her enemy. As I've said, she had a verbal velocity few could match.

Even when she was alone in the house she always had the radio on. She would routinely carry on conversations long after you left the room. My sister always said our mother didn't know how to be alone with her thoughts. I think she knew how; she just didn't *want* to be alone with them. She was a Pollyanna, as my father says, and when we are alone it is harder to keep our darker thoughts and anxieties at bay. Better to keep busy, drown them out with the thrum of daily living, than to sit quietly and think, reflect. Noise, like busyness, keeps the truth away.

In his emails my father explained that this lively, outspoken mother of mine – both versions of her – was unable to talk about sex. Not abstractly, not personally. She couldn't have a conversation about her own needs, desires, wants. Not even after being with this man since her late teens. On its own, this doesn't seem so strange. Repressed, not of the current trend perhaps, but no sign that something was deeply amiss.

In our emails that shot back and forth across the world in the wee hours of the morning, my father relayed more unusual details. My mother was a virgin when they met. This is what she told him, and it was physically confirmed – sex was painful, her hymen was very much intact. She had only one boyfriend before my father and insisted nothing had happened between them. But she was sexually experienced. She wanted and encouraged anal sex. Many years went by in which this was the only sexual act she would engage in. She was, as my father put it in his emails, oddly expert at this act. 'Whatever you've heard about the swinging sixties and seventies,' he wrote, 'that was not on the menu.' While he had always found this strange, he had never been able to discuss it with her. He had never had an explanation for it. I was not the only one unable to break her silence, to coax her into difficult or personal conversations.

With my revelations, these facts began to coalesce with others, building a story in his mind. She felt an overwhelming hostility towards her mother. In part, this centred on my grandmother's refusal to provide my mother with any sexual education. My father found her anger disproportionate. My grandmother was strangely protective of my mother, even though my mother was an adult and she and my father were deeply committed to one another. Once we progressed past emails, he explained over Skype that my grandmother had become terrifyingly and uncontrollably angry when he approached my grandparents about the two of them moving to Adelaide together in their twenties. My grandfather had to take my father out of the house, explain to him he had things to discuss with his wife and that they would revisit the conversation, then he disappeared inside to placate my raging grandmother. Her rage centred on her adult daughter being out of reach, out of sight.

This last story is, in large part, what made my father believe my grandmother knew something had happened to my mother but not acted. Had swept it under the rug, as was the custom in those days – particularly within families. Her reaction was so out of proportion, so dramatic, that in nearly forty years it never faded in my father's memory.

While I may have been close to my grandmother and found her understanding – insightful even – my mother's relationship with her was tense, difficult; they were unable to remain in the same room for more than an hour. In fact, it closely resembled the relationship between my mother and myself.

My father told me that many times he had to take my mother on a drive to let her cool off before returning to the house. Like that Möbius strip, history repeating in so many unfortunate ways.

Ultimately, through our discussions, my father concluded that my mother's early experiences of sex were indeed abusive. His next quest was to determine who was responsible. A boyfriend? he wondered, though my mother claimed to have had only one. A peer, perhaps? Certainly not her father, he concluded. After systematically ruling out other prominent men in her early life – ever the scientist – he settled on one.

'There is only one relative she constantly spoke about with revulsion,' he wrote in an email. 'He is my suspect. An uncle she said gave her the creeps and with whom the family spent a lot of time. I met the guy. He is my pick.'

I knew of that uncle too. She had spoken to me about him. On a trip home from a family reunion a few years before she died, she had called him a revolting man.

I also remembered something else. When I was about twelve or thirteen and starting to venture off unannounced – down the street to hang out with neighbourhood kids, into the city to hang out with school friends. I don't recall what prompted the conversation, but I remember sitting on the floor while my mother shifted from anger to distress. 'You don't know what it's like . . . to have someone, have men, pulling at your clothing. Doing things.' She wasn't completely coherent. At the time I didn't see how her comments had any relevance to me catching up with girlfriends to go to movies, or staying out later than I should. She said I was lucky I didn't have any men like that in my life, in my family. Though of course, I did have men in my life, if not my family. But this was before the letters.

———

I never thought I'd find myself in a detailed conversation about my parents' sex life with my father. But, then, it had been a year of words, sentences – whole paragraphs – I never thought I would say or hear. From 'my mother is dead', to 'I was sexually abused', and now 'I found out my mother was sexually abused because my father had an affair with a twenty-eight-year-old'.

A year in which the unthinkable became reality – mother dead, father an adulterer, husband gone. Secrets revealed.

'Don't,' I find myself whispering to the night, 'don't bring more pain. Don't take more from me.'

CHAPTER SIXTEEN

Finally, my mother's story

In the weeks and months after my mother died in February 2017, I had no regrets about my decision not to ask her the questions everyone wanted me to ask. That you, no doubt, wanted me to ask, to make sense of her actions. After her death I was many things – exhausted, shattered, transformed. But regretful was not one of them.

However, as I have learnt, not everyone is comfortable with unanswered questions. Not everyone is willing to find peace within themselves rather than search for answers elsewhere. While I felt no burning desire to hunt down the truth of my mother, through my father's searching, I arrived there, nonetheless.

Finally, my mother's story.

My mother was raised in a Catholic household. She hit her teens smack bang in the middle of the swinging sixties. The gap between her generation and her parents' cannot be measured in years. Culturally, it must be measured in worlds.

The first, my grandmother's, is the generation that grew up in the Depression, that went to war and never came back the same. The generation that did not know frivolity. My grandfather fought in the Second World War, my grandmother was a nurse based in Australia, treating returning soldiers.

They never spoke of the things they saw.

Known – appropriately – as the 'silent generation', they put their heads down, worked hard. They didn't challenge the status quo, they got on with rebuilding their lives as the country grew more prosperous, less desperate. They had families, went to church.

My mother's generation, coming of age in the 'Me decade', as Tom Wolfe called it, were considered self-involved, focused as they were on self-fulfilment, liberation and social change, unconcerned with family and social responsibility – at least in their youth. My mother and my grandmother were constantly at odds, over my mother's car rides with male friends, over short skirts and long hair. Maybe that doesn't seem like much, but it was deeply symbolic of changing times.

Sometime in these years, before she met my father at eighteen, something happened to my mother. Something not so different from what happened to me. And herein lies the truth of intergenerational trauma – when a child's trauma so closely parallels that of the parent, the parent is often rendered unable to act. Acting would mean reliving their own unprocessed trauma. It would mean doing something intolerable.

My mother's trauma was far from processed. In nearly forty years of marriage she never uttered a word of it to her husband.

For us millennials, a generation trained in signs of trauma – from think pieces, literature and memoir to community campaigns – it would have seemed obvious. To my father it did not, though all the signs were there:

- A woman who couldn't talk about sex, not even with her partner of four decades. Who would get angry when he tried.
- A woman who left the room when sexual violence was mentioned or presented on television.
- A woman who went into uncontrollable hysterics when her daughters went out alone with boys during their teenage years, or when adult men commented on their appearance.
- A woman who was secretive about her past, despite my father being the first man she ever had a sexual relationship with.

Small clues, yes. But enough that someone in my generation would guess that something more sinister lurked at the core of her youth than a Catholic mother.

There were larger clues too. I will come to those.

———

My grandmother had eight siblings. The youngest was her sister Miriam. Miriam's life is a tragic tale. Beautiful and young, she married the man my mother called 'revolting'. She had three children with her husband, who was known among the family to be very violent. One day her husband unceremoniously cast Miriam and their children out on the street. They turned up at another sister's house, asking to be taken in.

While still in her thirties, Miriam died of breast cancer. She left her children in the care of her new partner of just two years. This was highly unusual for the time, when children would normally have been returned to their father in the aftermath of their mother's death.

Miriam is the only woman in my family other than my mother to die of breast cancer. Though Miriam and my mother's lives are linked in more ways than just their deaths.

While I never knew Miriam, given she died many years before I was born, I met one of her children once. I had travelled with my mother to the tiny town of Carcoar, in the Central West of New South Wales, where my grandmother's family had settled upon arrival in Australia from Europe in the 1800s. It's a beautiful little town, untouched and largely forgotten – hours from anywhere. Nestled in a valley, with a red-brick railway station sitting on the hill – no longer used but perfectly maintained – and a creek running along the bottom. More like someone's private imagining than a real place.

We were there for a reunion of the Henn family, my grandmother's family, and Miriam's boy was there. I say 'boy', but this was around 2009; he would have been in his forties. Speaking with him made you want to treat him like a child, though. His fragility was so palpable you felt compelled to be gentle with him, soothing. He is a potter and, after we'd sat with him for a while at that reunion, he gave my mother and me each a piece of the most exquisite pottery you've ever seen. For me, a bowl. For my mother, a rusty earth-coloured tall thin vase. We cherished them both.

Driving home, my mother talked about Miriam's kids, about their terrible childhood. Their violent father, their mother dying when they were so terribly young. Had I known what I know now, I would have asked her far more on that two-hour drive from Carcoar to Canberra. Or at that family reunion, where 160 family members reunited to speak about the past. But not all of it.

Miriam's husband was more than physically violent to children. While I have enough facts to weave a narrative, I don't know the exact details of what happened to my mother. Maybe it was a boyfriend, maybe a different family member. But from what I do know, I believe it was that uncle. And I imagine it went something like this . . .

Cris's uncle was always an unwelcome presence, but Miriam was beloved by her sisters and they worried for her and her children, so they were always invited to family gatherings.

After consuming too much of the beer he brought for himself, Miriam's husband would get a little loose. He would make inappropriate jokes, comment on Miriam's sisters' looks. Especially, he would compliment Cris. Talk about her figure. How curvy she was for her age – just fifteen. How long and dark and thick her hair was.

Cris's mother would catch these comments, watch the pair of them out of the corner of her eye, but she carried on chatting with her sisters and their families, was distracted by the hordes of small children running around the table. Taking a little extra time with Charlie, Miriam's youngest, a timid little bird of a boy with bright red hair.

Cris's uncle would get frustrated and angry with Charlie, berating him harshly for spilling a drink, for forgetting to say thank you. He was less harsh with his daughters. They were quiet, careful . . . controlled. Obedient.

Cris he watched with a different kind of attention. There was a certain intensity to his gaze as he leant back in his chair, legs spread, a beer in one hand. Eyes following her around the room, around the table, across the yard.

Finally, my mother's story

He would watch and wait until the others were absorbed in banter, or tired from a long day of catching up in the sun. A few too many drinks, full bellies, worn-out children stretched out on the grass.

Then he would corner Cris alone. In a room. In a garage. In a part of the park that no one could see. He would stroke her arm, shift her long dark hair off her face. He would tell her she was beautiful. She is uncomfortable with his touch and starts to protest. He says, 'Shhhhhhhh, pretty girl.' He unbuckles his belt.

He kisses her roughly then turns her around, pulls at her clothes. Pushes himself painfully inside her, but not her vagina. No, he doesn't want to get caught by knocking up his young niece. Or maybe he just prefers it this way.

She goes quiet, numb. He finishes.

This scene repeats and repeats with every family gathering. Perpetually insecure about her weight and her looks, she both hates and enjoys this attention – being desired, being told she is beautiful by this man, is both awful and seductive. She too knows that feeling of fear and pleasure cohabiting in one body, control in someone else's.

Gradually, he begins to weave in threats.

'If you tell anyone, they'll all think you're a slut. No one will want to talk to you again. The family will hate you.'

'No one will believe you anyway, or if they do, they'll be furious at you for what you've done.'

He plays his cards perfectly, making use of the conservative Catholic culture of the family. She should be ashamed. Women are responsible for the acts of men. She is the filthy one here. She is the one who will be judged for her sins – sex before marriage, lust, sodomy.

Over a few years Cris's mother notices the tension between the two of them. Notices the way his eyes follow my young mother around the room, shifting down to her curvy rear when she bends over to pick up a plate or talk to a young cousin.

My grandmother's suspicions intensify. Her daughter is secretive. Her brother-in-law too comfortable when he touches her daughter on the shoulder, on the arm, around the waist. Cris's mother senses something intimate in that touch, something not right.

Still, she says nothing.

With time, she manoeuvres her brother-in-law out of Cris's life. They stop attending gatherings where he will be present. They do not see him or his three children anymore. They do not speak of any of this. It is dealt with.

Many years later, one of Miriam's daughters commits suicide at twenty-five.

Cris reaches out to the other daughter whom she remembers fondly. They don't speak of what happened but Cris offers her a home. She offers her safety, she offers her family.

She recognises a shared suffering and trauma between

them – something she was unable to do for her daughter. Perhaps, having buried her trauma deeper and deeper with the passage of time, her capacity for solidary was lost.

Now you know.

Do you feel differently now? Can you excuse her? Do you still judge her?

For me, this knowledge doesn't change anything fundamental. I had guessed she must have carried a similar trauma to me to act the way she did. Yet knowing her story makes my story sadder, I feel. I am now part of a lineage of women who have failed their daughters. A lineage of fractured, difficult relationships, underpinned by lies, denial and violence.

But as I write these words I look at the gold band I wear on my finger. It belonged to my grandmother, then my mother, now me. People think I wear it to remember them both. I do, but not in the way you might think. I wear it to remind myself that they did the best they could – for their generation, within the cultural and social norms of their times. My grandmother's a time when sexual abuse was a family shame you swept under the rug. My mother's a time when psychologists and counselling meant you were mentally ill and stigmatised.

I wear the ring to remind myself that I can do better. That I can move through life not unaffected by trauma, but able to speak about it. I don't have to wrap it up in shame and hide it out of view. This is because I live in a different time and, although I may carry similar scars to the women in my family who came before me, I am not them. I have worn this ring ever since discovering my mother's secret. It reminds me that I am part of a story of intergenerational abuse, violence and destructive silence that can end with me. That my grandmother and mother were as strong as they could be, but I am stronger.

CHAPTER SEVENTEEN

Chasing ghosts

As Patti Smith says, 'Sometimes you're doing really well, then, after three or four years, everything inexplicably crashes like a house of cards and you have to rebuild it.' But how do you go about rebuilding a house when every wall has been torn down, by your own hand or another's?

One way to try to rebuild is to dig deeper. Create space for new foundations. Start from the bottom up, as it were.

For me, this meant seeking out what I could about my mother's life. I did not ask her about the letters, and I have no regrets – to this day I do not believe she could have spoken about her own trauma, which would have been the only way she could explain her actions truthfully or satisfactorily. But with the outline I had from my father, I felt I needed to go looking for the rest of her story.

It's a difficult thing to uncover intimate details of abuse when those involved are dead. It's even more difficult when you take into account the silence that surrounds sexual abuse, particularly when my mother was young. And especially when it might involve a family member. You are left chasing ghosts.

I had only a few clues. An uncle, now dead. Just two family members still alive, distant and belonging to my grandmother's generation or my mother's.

Still, I tracked them down. And, they shut me down. I spoke first to one of my mother's cousins, whom I have known my whole life. She told me that she was disturbed by my enquiry. Disturbed that I was hunting for the truth of something. Something from the depths of the past. 'There is nothing I can say or do to help you.'

Next, I reached out to the cousin who had stayed with my mother when they were young. She said nothing of the violence in her family, even though it is legendary across my mother's side of the family. 'Henn women are strong, they just get on with things,' she chirped, which seemed to be her way regardless of the topic. 'Besides, your grandmother was so foreign to us. She was beautiful and poised and unapproachable. No one would question her judgement.' By this, she meant that no one would dare suggest my grandmother would allow something untoward to occur on her watch. But that poise, that sense of 'the proper way to do things' – the proper way to be – is precisely the type of facade erected to keep secrets and transgressions hidden.

We have family friends whom I call my cousins, though we're not related by blood. I call them my cousins because we go back three generations, our grandmothers posted together to the middle of nowhere – the Hay Plains – during the war. The next generation went to school together, while my generation spent summers at the beach – hours whiled away in the surf and playing backyard cricket. Reflecting on the oldest of the three generations, my mother's best friend said to me once, 'You only ever saw what they wanted you to see of them,' hinting that there was a great deal more to them than any of us would ever know.

In all the interactions with my mother's family, I felt the heavy weight of silence, and of having broken family and generational rules by asking such direct questions. Here I was again, throwing truth in the face of silence and denial.

Neither of the two distant family members I spoke to said they would think about it further, neither offered to help me on my search for answers. They merely said 'no'. Even the one I've known all my life, who promised to visit me in Canberra, has never spoken to me again.

Those answers – rebuttals, really – were too quick off the mark. There was no pondering, no 'let me think about this', 'let me help you search for the truth of your mother'. There were no disclosures of family secrets and struggles I already knew of from my mother on our long drive to and from the family reunion. The violence, children thrown out of the home. There was just a wall of silence.

It's frustrating not to be able to reconstruct the puzzle. To know beyond any doubt that your suspicions – the who, the what, the how – are correct. But dealing with trauma, searching out the dark heart of it, also carries responsibility. I felt this responsibility when I considered reaching out to other victims of David in the months after my mother was diagnosed, and after David and I exchanged our last words.

I felt it again when I spoke to my mother's family.

Just because I have decided to seek answers does not give me the right to re-traumatise others. In the case of my abuser, many of the girls were older – though not by much. What if they saw their experiences with him as misguided but not necessarily abusive? What would it do to them to hear he was a child sex offender? If they escaped him with minimal damage, I feel strongly that I have no right to create trauma in their lives in my search to come to terms with my own.

This holds true for my mother's family. I know the women in my family I spoke to had suffered violence at the hands of men. Yet they didn't offer this information up to me when I enquired about my mother, no matter how gently, how carefully, I approached the subject. And so I did not probe too much further.

I have come to realise over the course of my mother's dying and the revelations that followed that I do not have the right to do others damage because I want the truth. This was the logic I applied to my mother, and why I never asked her about the letters or shared my suspicion that she had experienced sexual abuse. Sometimes there are things people simply can't talk about. Sometimes we shouldn't try to make them.

You may find this unsatisfying. You may feel that I should hunt down the facts, push these women for answers, their feelings be damned. But as someone who has experienced complex trauma, I feel determined to ensure it stops with me. To do no harm, as it were. And I do not know enough about the journeys of these women to determine whether it would be safe for them to discuss things long buried. As it was not safe for my mother.

'Many people live and die without ever confronting themselves in the darkness,' as Carmen Maria Machado writes in her short story 'The Resident'. While she was not speaking of trauma, her words ring true in this context also. I believe we have no right to make people confront themselves and their past, even when it might help others transcend their own. It must be a choice we arrive at ourselves. A journey we *choose* to take, not one thrust upon us by others.

This question applies as much to readers as it does to me. What right does a reader have to expect women to expose themselves to trauma, or re-traumatise themselves, for the sake of completeness?

I am not the first to pose this question. Laura Bennett of *Slate*, former *Gawker* editor Emily Gould and Jia Tolentino, former deputy editor of *Jezebel*, are just some of the women who have asked these same questions of themselves and others. For a time, Laura Bennett argues, the internet was taken over by first-person essays. The more dramatic, traumatic – sensational, from a marketing perspective – the better. Natasha Chenier wrote about having sex with her father, Lidia Yuknavitch about being raped while unconscious, having passed out from drugs, when living rough under a bridge.

Writing these types of personal essays is a delicate act. A tightrope of social responsibility. Yes, voices must be heard. Difficult, confronting, violent stories need to be told. If they are not, we fail to break the cultures of silence and shame that surround these actions, these acts of violence. I agree with Audre Lorde's staunch arguments against silence. Speaking about racialised trauma, she wrote in 'The Transformation of Silence into Language and Action': 'Your silences will not protect you.' She asked, 'What are the words you do not yet have? What are the tyrannies you swallow day by day and attempt to make your own, until you will sicken and die of them, still in silence?' Yet in writing my mother's story, and to a lesser extent my own, I have wondered: What do I owe you as a reader?

Do you need every salacious detail?

Every stomach-churning moment of what it is to live through and with abuse?

Or is it enough to know the outline? To hear instead about the ways in which these events can flow through every part of people's lives, and on to other generations. In the words of Audre Lorde again: 'I have a duty to speak the truth as I see it and share not just my triumphs, not just the things that felt good, but the pain, the intense, often unmitigated pain. It is important to share how I know survival is survival and not just a walk.' But can we describe and do justice to that pain, that walk, without describing every wound, every step, in the greatest of detail?

If I were to scour the six metres of bookshelves that line the walls of my current home and pull out the books that convinced me I would survive the entwined traumas of abuse, death and betrayal – and give them to you – it would be a small pile. Obscure, and not for everyone in their unflinching accounts. But those books do more than lay out the facts for you – a chronology of events. They *show* you the contradictions that exist in trauma and grief, they show you the walk.

Here, you can listen to Meghan Daum tell you how she wished her mother would hurry up and die. That she looked up momentarily from the book she was reading when her mother took her last breath and remarked aloud, 'Is that it?' And you'll realise that you are not the only woman who grapples with a mixture of grief and relief when her mum is dead.

Take a winding journey with Sarah Manguso. Trace your steps back to every moment – every conversation, every action – in your life where you might have done something different. Changed the course of events.

With Lidia Yuknavitch, there will be urinating on supermarket floors, sobbing fully clothed in showers. There will be sex and alcohol and mistakes, as you see how she scratches out a life for herself, finally. One that is full of meaning.

These are the stories that have helped me to come to terms with my own story of intergenerational abuse. Yes, that means meeting yourself in the darkness, but it does not necessarily follow that *everything* we find in that darkness needs to be revealed to others. Take Lidia Yuknavitch, for example, who writes uncompromisingly of her struggles with family, addiction, violence. *The Chronology of Water* is a deeply confronting and moving piece of memoir and art, but it does not delve into the heart of what caused Yuknavitch's struggles in gory detail. Only once does she say she was sexually abused by her father. This most intimate of traumas is not dissected; not laid bare for the reader to wince and squirm at. Instead, she shows us how it flowed into every part of her life – every crevice, every experience. And in doing so, she teaches us how she learnt to live with it.

That Yuknavitch shows us her survival, but does it without taking us to the darkest of her traumas, is, I believe, where the true power of her book lies. Through those actions, she shows her readers – and the world – that it's okay to be a 'misfit'; someone who missed fitting in. It's okay to have felt that you are not quite normal because you have secrets; secrets that mean you have to figure out how to put yourself back together in such a way that you will 'fit'. And that, in the meantime, this can make you seem wild and chaotic. And, finally, it's okay that it can take a long time to find the words to tell these stories. But there can be something transformational about both finding them and organising them on the page, or in your mouth, in the way *you* want. Which can also mean leaving a few out.

While I dug into my mother's past, I stopped short where I felt that pushing women in my family further would cause them damage. I know I will never be fully myself, will never be content, if I stay silent. But I know that my story rubs up against, at times winds in and out of, the stories of others, some of which are not mine to tell. Some of which I have no right to ask about or commit to the page. Emily Gould, in her *New York Times Magazine* essay 'Exposed', reached a similar conclusion after years of writing about her personal life and considering the effects of her writing on those whose lives were intertwined with hers. 'I kept coming back to the idea that I had a right to say whatever I wanted [but] I don't think I understood then that I could be right about being free to express myself but wrong about my right to make that self-expression public in a permanent way.'

What does this leave me with?

It leaves me with a sketch of what happened to my mother. But it also leaves me with a heightened awareness of the silence that surrounds sexual violence.

You could argue, though, that silence is in many ways far more central to this story than the exact details of my mother's abuse. I believe in the version of events I have painted here. But I am also acutely aware how strong the culture of silence is around sexual abuse. As renowned trauma therapist Judith Herman writes, secrecy and silence are the perpetrator's allies – their first line of defence.

When I spoke to my mother's cousin, she suggested that if my mother had never spoken of her abuse, this was evidence it had not happened. I didn't speak of my abuse for twenty years, I wanted to say. Believe me. It happened.

Silence is not evidence of the absence of an event. Silence is evidence of a culture of repression and shame concerning sexual violence. Silence is what needs to be written about. Needs to be broken. Or we will all be caught in this awful endless loop. But, still, it must be handled delicately.

In my family, this silence has played out through generations. It may even stretch back before my mother.

Chasing ghosts

My grandmother, one of nine children, was twice sent away from her family for years – once before school and then later as a teenager. Who knows what happened to her during these stays with distant family members and places? This story may have begun earlier still – stretching back further than I can ever know.

The silence around sexual abuse that has flowed through generations of my family created the conditions for my own abuse. Here I stand, three generations deep, and that silence is still causing harm. Silence is not passive. Silence can be the most powerful and destructive of acts. To this day I am unable to bear witness to things – at home, in workplaces, anywhere – and not speak out. Silence has become my enemy. And so, I chose to break it. Both when I was seventeen, and then, twenty years after the abuse began, here in this book. But I must learn to temper my hatred of silence with the needs of others. Not everyone wishes, or is able, to live their life out loud.

When I think about this pervasive culture of silence that is only beginning to change, it makes me realise just how incredible it is that I managed to take David to court. Not just that I broke the silence at a time when it was so much harder to do so, but that people *listened*. That he was, initially, convicted by a jury.

The day that Cardinal George Pell was found guilty by the jury for sexual abuse of a minor in 2019 on the evidence of just one alleged victim, speaking out later, I cried in my office. Looking out the window at the large elm tree that stretches over the university quad below, I took in the green of the leaves and the blue of the sky.

In that moment I close my eyes and imagine him standing in a witness box, a far statelier one than where David met his judgement, telling his story. I imagine the dinner he will have with his family later that night; how the room will smell of tears and champagne. And I imagine how he will lie in bed after it's over, while his wife sleeps beside him, wondering how on earth his life has led him here.

How can you feel such an affinity with someone you've never seen? Whose name you don't even know? Whose voice you've never heard? You can because you know, *you know*, that same peculiar muddle of sadness, relief and validation. Ultimately, of a righteousness you wish was not yours to own.

Maybe that day brought him the same lightness that came over me when my literary agent said she wanted to make sure a great many people read this book. It radiated out from my chest, through my limbs and floated dizzyingly into my head; this realisation that my whole life I had felt as though I had been followed by a name, and soon that feeling would be gone. Until that point, I had carried David's name with me everywhere I went. There are several famous people who share it; when I would see it in credits on movie screens, which happens every now and then, my breath would catch. While friends sat peacefully in the dark of the cinema, I'd be thrown backwards to 1995. But when people know, the shame lands where it belongs: in my case on the perpetrator. You don't have to carry someone else's name – someone else's crimes – everywhere you go.

While the media and friends jumped straight to the questions of Pell's appeal and the fights over 'truth' that would follow, I pleaded over social media: 'Take a moment. Sit with the fact that one of the most powerful men in the world was at that time found guilty because one victim, who had no witnesses, was not only listened to, but believed by a jury.' Appreciate that this is stunning – even though this jury verdict was eventually overturned by the High Court.

Looking back with the wisdom of years, my story seems nearly impossible.

———

So, yes, I dug into the past in an attempt to rebuild my life – to draw the truth out of the silences. But I had limits about how hard I pushed the women I spoke to. I may know more than when I decided to let my mother die with the secrets that bound us, but I still choose to live with a certain amount of ambiguity concerning what happened to her; an ambiguity mirrored by the ways in which breaking silence can be both healing and harmful in different contexts, for different people. Frustrating though it may be to some, ambiguity is the stuff that lives are made of, and, as it turns out, deaths.

CHAPTER EIGHTEEN

The outline of a man we used to know

I wonder, what does a father owe his daughters in the aftermath of their mother's death?

Empathy? Practicality? Care?

Perhaps nothing. Perhaps I owe him nothing in return.

———

My sister and I are book shopping. She is back from Boston briefly and many months have passed since my mother's death. She's been worried about my father and me, and rightly so. She came back to try to mend things a little, and the three of us decide to head down to the South Coast once again, emulating our family tradition. Pretending things are the same, or trying to rebuild, I'm not sure.

In the bookshop, she and I both gather piles of books in our arms and head to the counter. I suggest we cross-check; maybe we don't need so many.

'Do any of yours have pirates?' she asks.

'No,' I reply. 'Are any of yours brutally honest memoirs or about family betrayal?'

As I said, we don't believe we actually share any DNA.

While we're waiting at the register my sister picks up a book on display – *Extinctions*, by Josephine Wilson. She reads the back cover, laughs, and hands it to me. The blurb reads:

> His wife is dead, and his two adult children are lost to him in their own ways. Surrounded and obstructed by the debris of life – objects he has collected over many years and tells himself he is keeping for his daughter – he is determined to be miserable, but is tired of his existence and the life he has chosen.

We stare at each other and laugh, because what else can you do in those moments when you realise your own life has become stranger than fiction?

'Too close to home,' my sister says.

'Like someone just wrote about our family's last year . . . I kind of want to buy it, and I kind of want to burn it,' I replied.

We leave it on the shelf.

The outline of a man we used to know

After learning about my father, I began reading more about grief to try to understand his behaviour. Ever the researcher, I tried to research the problem away.

What did I learn?

While grief is natural, when we do not process it – when we pretend it isn't happening – paradoxically our attempts to make it small instead make it grow. Grief begins to colonise us, reaching into every corner of our mind and personality – altering us, sometimes beyond recognition or repair.

In states of traumatic grief, grief shifts from something devastatingly painful but necessary to something more insidious. It becomes amorphous and uncontainable. It becomes unhealthy, so the clinicians tell us, as though clear distinctions can be drawn about something so deeply individual.

When a person suffers traumatic grief, they avoid reminders of the deceased. They behave strangely and inappropriately. They may cry or yell at seemingly random moments. They may have unpredictable bursts of anger, which are disproportionate to the issue at hand.

Their grief is trying to climb its way out.

It is demanding to be heard.

But because the person won't let it, it makes itself known in unexpected ways – often without any awareness by the owner of that grief, strange as this may sound.

As anyone who has faced grief knows, you cannot run from it, you cannot hide from it. Grief, the pain of it, is important – you need to succumb to it in order to deal with it. In order to transcend it. You cannot deny it away, ignore it away, drink it away or distract it away.

This, however, is exactly what my father tried to do.

At first, he hid from his grief in the arms of his young mistress. While she was in his life, from the outside all was calm. In weeks and early months after my mother's death he cooked meals. He would spend hours following one of a handful of recipes he'd been perfecting in the year my mother was dying – proving he would be able to take care of himself once she was gone. He'd proudly set the meal down on the table – seared tuna, or a risotto – and lay out plywood placemats, hand-printed with patterns by an artist whose studio was on my street in Melbourne. Following the rituals of my mother.

And we would sit across from each other and talk about politics.

In those early months, he carried on. It felt as though things would be okay – *he would be 'okay'*.

When I found out about his mistress and gave him that ultimatum, I dragged him back to the ugliness of his life.

A dead wife.

Daughters struggling with their own grief, one of them in the midst of divorce.

The pressure of creating, of being, 'family'.

I anchored him to that grief. No, there would be no escape for my father in the arms of a young woman – I had seen to that.

After his mistress was gone, he tried to research his grief away, though in a different way from me. It was as though if he could just understand why my mother, of all people, had died of an uninheritable, hideously aggressive form of breast cancer, with no known causes, he could put the matter to rest. He picked at the medical literature at random – drawing erroneous links between various illnesses she had suffered in her life, suggesting they ultimately had led to the cancer.

He searched for clues as to whether my sister and I would suffer the same fate – though, as we swiftly pointed out, the issue was moot. There was no cure and, having witnessed the so-called treatment firsthand, we weren't interested.

'If I get her cancer, I am going to go live it up on an island somewhere in South-East Asia and probably just drown myself in the sea before it gets really bad,' replied my sister.

She wasn't joking. That is precisely what she would do. I wouldn't accept the treatment either, but I'd more likely hunker down with loved ones and have long fraught emotional chats with them about death.

When we rebuffed his research, he buried himself in administrative tasks – often manufactured; did he really need to concern himself with the economic security of the next forty years of my life and my sister's?

'When there's nothing else to work himself up about, there's always money,' my sister sighed.

I'd never really understood this about my father until I read *One Hundred Years of Dirt*, Rick Morton's memoir about poverty and class in Australia. As he explains, regardless of how your circumstances change, whatever wealth and comfort you might accumulate, you know that all you have amassed can be gone in a moment. And you remember what that life was like. Your knowledge of poverty isn't abstract – something you've read about or, in my case, researched. It is, as he puts it, 'curled around your DNA'.

People like me, who grew up in a comfortable middle-class home, always have a sense of safety net; family, networks, favours owed. Poverty is a faraway land you've looked at through a telescope, and in my case spent your adult life fighting to end in no doubt 'elite' sorts of ways, but it isn't somewhere you've actually visited. Over coffee one cold Canberra morning, I told Rick that his book had made me understand my father more than over thirty years of talking to him.

Still, my sister and I gently mocked our father for his endless calculations, usually sent after midnight. When he emailed my sister to tell her that she should probably look at selling the beach house by 2090, based on his calculations of projected sea level rise due to climate change, we each received a calendar invite from her: December 2085 – 'Discuss plans for beach house'.

The research, the administration, didn't offer the same salve as his mistress. Once she was gone, he gave up the pretence of normality. No more cooking. No more carefully arranged placemats, conversational dinners. My parents' large wine collection disappeared at rapid speed; we learnt to hide the gin before he arrived at dinner parties.

Even when he was in the same room as us, he was palpably absent. Silences were interrupted by bouts of profuse swearing. Sitting in the living room I'd suddenly hear him yell, 'You motherfucking cunt!' Aimed at no one. Aimed, probably, at the whole goddamn world.

Often the outbursts were brought about by administrative tasks associated with my mother's dying. Tasks that seemed to drag on and on, almost endlessly and certainly beyond what anyone would deem reasonable.

What happens to those who die and have no one to take care of the mountains of paperwork? Sometimes that thought genuinely keeps me up at night, I have been so perplexed by the bureaucratic complexity of her death.

For the most part his swearing distressed me. But not always.

One afternoon a hospital bill for my mother arrived via email – for a scan that was done the day before she died. A scan that showed the tissue in her abdomen was bloated with fluid – a sure sign of near death. The bill came with a letter warning that if it wasn't paid soon it would affect her credit rating. After one of his strings of profanities, Dad called out as he typed: 'Cris is dead. She doesn't give a *fuck* about her credit rating,' and hit send. From across the room I began laughing, and shortly my father joined in.

Again, sometimes all you can do in the dark times of your life is laugh. To this day, I enjoy recounting, 'If they're too young for me to fuck, Dad, they're certainly too young for you to fuck,' at dinner parties, relishing in the black humour.

———

This chaotic, grasping search for control is what traumatic grief looks like. My sister and I refer to the months after my mother's death – once I had disposed of his mistress – as my father's 'psychotic period'. While he and I were largely estranged during this time, he rang my sister relentlessly to discuss the same things over and over – forgetting they had already spoken of them. We feared for his mental health. Even when my sister came back for Christmas at the end of 2017, a full ten months after my mother's death, she could hear my father through the wall of his bedroom yelling obscenities in his sleep. Obscenities that were beyond what she could bring herself to repeat to me – and my sister is no shrinking violet.

No matter how forcefully my father insisted he was fine, that he had it all under control, in sleep his body betrayed him. His grief demanded to be known. It demanded to be heard.

My father isn't a rare case. Clinically, traumatic grief is thought to occur to 10 per cent of bereaved people, though grief itself is believed to be responsible for 15 per cent of psychiatric referrals, as psychotherapist Julia Samuel notes in her book *Grief Works*. Traumatic grief is described as a sense of anger, yearning or feelings of being stuck that lasts more than six months. It occurs when people try to block or fight the experiences of grief.

Samuel describes grief as the challenge of living with a terrible paradox – we must find a way to survive in a reality which we do not wish to be true. There is a persistent belief that we can 'fix just about anything and make it better', writes Samuel. 'Grief is the antithesis of this belief: it eschews avoidance and requires endurance, and forces us to accept that there are some things in this world that simply cannot be fixed.'

So it was, in the months after my mother's death, my father developed traumatic grief. With his refusal to seek help or admit there was a problem, all my sister and I could do was try to buffer ourselves against its chaos. Where once there had been my father – emotionally limited but smart, capable, rational – stood a stranger.

The outline of a man we used to know.

———

The house, for a time, fell into disrepair. The beautiful garden my mother had planted all but died. The fish disappeared from their pond. New animals appeared – small plagues running rampant in different parts of the house.

This is what happens when you inhabit a house, but it ceases to be a home.

My father's and my relationship fell into disrepair too. It shifted unpredictably between awkwardness, silence, fury and declarations that we were done with one another. Sometimes I sat and cried about, and for my mother, for hours. Always in the living room, he would sit on the couch opposite me again, usually staring at his feet, muttering the odd platitude. Clearly helpless in the face of my grief and sadness. Changed though it was, I still belonged to a family where emotion is weakness, or at the very least something that shouldn't be put on open display.

Even when I wrote a piece for *The Guardian* on the grief of losing my mother, my father struggled to acknowledge it. It didn't delve into the more complex and challenging parts of our relationship but instead spoke only of the sadness. I received emails from strangers on the other side of the world. Friends and colleagues stopped me when they saw me and said how it had made them cry. The morning it was published he called out to my sister, who was back from America again, 'Did you see what Gem wrote?'

He never spoke of it again.

———

In these months, my father tried to show me he cared in the only way he could. I had moved into my own house in

The outline of a man we used to know

June 2017 – finally the build was done. It was a thing of beauty; an eco-house with clean lines and walls of glass. My father and I had designed it together, way back before my mother got sick. One afternoon we stood on the pavement with half the neighbourhood and watched our design come to life. Pre-built rooms were lifted into place by an enormous crane, and then a roof was rolled over the top. After living in one room for more than a year, waiting, my house appeared in three days.

I immediately set about making it mine – filling it with things dragged out from storage, along with the pre-emptive housewarming gifts my mother had given me.

I was building my new home and my new life all at once.

I chose to line the walls with bookshelves.

I designed the joinery in every room, down to my custom-made three-metre floating wooden desk that looks out over the garden.

I chose it all, and I asked no one for permission.

My father played his own role in this rebuilding. With my limited physical strength and the chronic pain I suffer in my hands, the garden was beyond me.

He spent hours laying paving, planning the contours of garden beds. I like to think it was his way of trying to make up for what he couldn't give emotionally. For the burden I had carried for him, and the toll it had taken.

In the garden, we could talk. While we worked at the periphery of my home, our conversations stayed light.

I suppose there's little chance that emotions will come up when you're planning the layout of a hedge, laying paving or discussing drought-proof plants.

He rarely, if ever, entered my house.

Despite the tentative truce we had forged, flare-ups still occurred. Particularly when my sixty-eight-year-old father would temporarily be taken over by a fourteen-year-old boy.

A few times, after working on the garden, he would come inside. Have a drink with people who happened to have stopped by. Sure enough, given time, a series of inappropriate comments would be made about someone's sex life, young women or women's bodies.

The worst of these happened, at a dinner party with our closest friends, at that big long table at their house where he teased his mate about being a 'minor god'.

I arrive late that night, and my father and his friend are already a few glasses of wine down. We stand milling around the long wooden table, chatting. I announce I've been headhunted and now shortlisted for a senior role at a well-known research centre, which would mean a promotion to associate professor. If offered the role, I explain, this would make me one of the youngest women in the country to have achieved such a success.

My father scoffs a little. 'It's a long shot, Gem. You're not going to get it.'

'Thanks for the vote of confidence, Dad,' I respond.

The outline of a man we used to know

But this isn't what hurt me that night.

After his remark about my poor chances at securing a high-profile job, he moves on to discuss his dating life. Tells us all how many young women are showing an interest in him. He smirks, sips his red wine, and says offhandedly, 'You shouldn't drop by the house unannounced, Gem.' I can't decide if he's telling the truth or just showing off to his friend – the one with whom he is forever caught in a game of one-upmanship.

I lower my gaze. I try not to cry, though I can feel the tears building up.

'That isn't appropriate, Alan,' I say, but he doesn't see the hurt. Hurt is no longer visible to him – hiding from his own pain has made that of others' invisible.

He laughs.

One of our friends, more attuned to the tension, says, 'You only do this because you love each other.'

Neither my father nor I say anything. We let the conversation move on, while I wonder, 'Do we love each other? Does this new version of my father love me?'

I excuse myself early from the dinner party. I drive to a friend's place, where we huddle on the living room floor by the only heater, his house made from paper-thin walls. I let myself cry while I retell the story. Once I reach the end, I grab my phone:

> If you think that young women will ever be a source of entertainment and humour you have completely failed

> to understand the depth of hurt and betrayal you have caused my sister and me.

The next day, a text back:

> I'm sorry.

Apologies have always been rare in my family. There were apology gifts, apology dinners, apology outings. But rarely an actual apology. A straight-up 'I am sorry'. So I don't for a minute think it wasn't sincere. It's the only time I remember him saying those words – I'm sorry – in my whole life. But still, the callousness was more than I could forgive. Even if my father becomes a man we recognise again, which he gradually is, some things we will be unable to forget. As with my mother, some hurts run too deep. We just put them to one side instead.

At one point in those months, back on his couches, I asked my father what, if he hadn't wanted to be married to my mother for fifteen years, was he mourning?

'A life half lived. Cut short by pain.'

Personally, I doubt that this is completely true. If it were, why was he so unmoored? To me, he felt like a man missing half of himself. He may not have wanted to be married to her at the end, but their life together was long. They travelled the world, they saw each other through the deaths of their parents, they had two children.

He was mourning her. We all were. In all her imperfections.

But by this point, six months after my mother's death, I was drained. I was done. I couldn't keep imploring him to behave like the man we used to know. Or even a man I wanted to know.

As my sister watched me struggle, she began to step into bat for the father we used to know – to try to bring him back. Much of it happened in private conversations, exchanges I wasn't privy to. But I do know that when my father announced he didn't want to do anything for Christmas, didn't want it to 'turn into a wake' for my mother, it was my sister who took him on.

'Yeah, 'cause her memory has been treated with so much respect this year, God forbid we take some time to remember her.'

She then went about organising a Christmas lunch, a tree like we had every year. She decorated it with the same decorations my mother used; a mixture of expensive glass balls and those dog-eared ugly odds and ends we all seem to accumulate over decades of Christmases.

She filled the house with the smell of fresh pine, bringing us back to our childhoods. Finally, she brought out a present my mother, she and I had bought for Dad the year before: a giant jigsaw puzzle to take to the coast, as was the family tradition. She put it under the tree. A great big silver box with our father's name on it, bought by his dead wife, taking centre place. Like a giant 'fuck you' to his attempts to shut her out, to erase her.

Through these acts, my sister set about rebuilding our family, making the family house home again.

———

I thought the year of cancer was the most brutal I would ever experience.

I was wrong.

The year that followed was harder. I was completely unprepared for what grief would do to each of us, and what we would do to each other as a result.

Large chunks of time are missing from my memory again – just like they are from my childhood.

I struggled in ways I never have before.

My mother and I had a difficult relationship, but her early death by cancer does not negate the fact that it is still a tragedy. My mother's death is every bit as heartbreaking as anyone else's. It is also more complex. I had to grieve the mother I had and the mother I wished I had had. People who learnt of the darker elements of our relationship frequently didn't understand this complexity.

Most of all, I had hoped that, in the space that opened up when she died, we could create a new family dynamic. That the closeness my father and sister and I had developed while caring for her would continue – would grow and flourish into the family I had always hoped for. That old family narratives would be disrupted once and for all.

I guess when it comes to our parents, or our longing for them to be a certain way, we can all be a little naive. I didn't get the family I had always dreamt of through my mother's death. Life doesn't work that way – taking one thing away but handing you something you always yearned for in return. Instead, once my mother's gravity was gone, we all scattered to the wind. We became three strangers who kept accidentally hurting each other. Forget the family I wished I'd always had, for much of that year there was no family at all.

And in so many ways my father picked up exactly where my mother left off. The callous comments. The sweeping of my sexual abuse under the rug – after Budapest we never spoke of it again. The shutting down of emotions. As though the family dynamic was so deeply entrenched it implored that those still standing reach down, pick it up and carry it on, even if they'd never liked it to begin with.

CHAPTER NINETEEN

Now you are gone

I wrote letters to my mother during this time. Little snapshots of things I partly wished she could see but mostly was relieved she couldn't.

'Death is the great exposer: it forces hidden fault lines and submerged secrets into the open, and reveals to us how crucial those closest to us have been,' writes Samuel in *Grief Works*. My mother's death had pushed the secrets of both of us into the open, but along with them a love that was not always apparent when she still had breath.

People close to us act as mirrors. They help us to know ourselves, to understand ourselves, even if it is through railing against the distorted image they reflect back at us. As though we are trying to force a circus mirror into a regular one – make a truer, more accurate, reflection of ourselves in their eyes. Or at least what we believe to be a truer reflection.

What do you do when one of those mirrors breaks? Despite our difficulties, my mother and I always talked.

I miss her in the silences she has left behind. The ones she would have filled with chatter – both meaningful and meaningless. I understand now, in a way I did not before, that even the meaningless is in fact meaningful.

Around eighteen months after my mother's death, I was travelling again for work. Some colleagues and my new partner and I rented a house to stay in while attending a conference in Edinburgh. It was snowing outside much of the time, and we huddled under blankets in the living room around an unlit fireplace. Tucked into the frame of a mirror above the fireplace was a postcard. On the postcard, a person, sketched in black and white, stood alone on a hill. In bold, written across the top: 'Her absence filled the world.'

'Yes,' I thought, 'it does.'

So much had happened I would have talked to my mother about. Instead I could only write her letters – letters she could never read.

It's useless to tell someone who is grieving that it is natural. That it is something everyone will face eventually. Everyone's grief is qualitatively different; it comes in different flavours, I have discovered, and I cannot explain my particular grief in all its complex shades and hues to those around me. While I know that my grief is unknowable, still I sought to know it as intimately as I could. And so I tried to capture it in letters. I tried to capture her *absence* in letters, as if such a thing were possible.

Dear Mum,
Your ashes came today.
    They are so heavy.
    Too heavy for me to lift.
    You were too heavy for me to lift up, in life or in death.
    Love,
    Gem

Dear Mum,
When people ask about how my father is coping, I reply, 'No one can save someone else from their own grief.'
    Why do I think this doesn't apply to me?
    Love,
    Gem

Dear Mum,
While your husband is away, travelling for work, I have come back to his house. To your house. Your illness and death created only a temporary pause in his transience.
    The house is full of rats. They run out from under the fridge across the room. They scuttle through the roof, making the dog growl.

Now you are gone so many other creatures are making a home here.

Someone has to. My father is not making a home here. He is simply passing time.

Love,
Gem

———

Dear Mum,
I'm sorry.

I know that I always wanted you to be sorry. Sorry for all the hurt you caused. Sorry for taking all my hurt and making it yours. I think in your own way you were sorry.

I think it would have hurt you to leave, to allow yourself to die, if you'd known this is what would happen to us all. I promised you we'd be okay. Right now we are not okay. Not in ourselves, or together. I feel I have broken my promise to you. Even if you had no right to ask it of me – to place such a burden on your youngest child.

Love,
Gem

———

Dear Mum,
For all that was hard and painful between us, I wish you were here.

I wish I had known the truth of your life while you

still had breath. The truth that you, like me, **were** abused then betrayed by your mother. But I also **know** that was never possible. That this is the only way it **could** be. And so here I am.

Love,
Gem

———

Dear Mum,
A woman at the electricity complaints department cried for you today, when she heard the cancer had taken you. You had, it seems, achieved the impossible – made a stranger care about you while complaining to her.

I didn't know what to do with this stranger's grief. I thanked her for it.

When I hung up the phone I cried too. I don't know if it was for her, for you or for me.

Love,
Gem

———

Dear Mum,
This week my father finally worked out how to remove your voice from the answering machine. It only took us three months.

I wonder if we will miss it: 'Hi, you've reached the Careys. We can't get to the phone right now but leave a message and we'll call you back. Bye for now.'

'Bye for now.' That phrase. I used to scoff when it played. Now it has taken on new meaning.

We might miss it. But hearing it every time we failed to make it to the phone in time stopped us in our tracks. Placed our hearts in our mouths.

And so it had to go.

Love,

Gem

———

Dear Mum,

I realise now I had a lot to work through. It took a marriage. It took a divorce. It took a death.

Sometimes I think I'm ready for the future. Other times I suspect there will be more to work through. Though these are not mutually exclusive.

Love,

Gem

———

Dear Mum,

I've lost count of all the forms of transport I've cried on. Buses, aeroplanes, trains. And some objects that don't move. Desks, tables.

Will this river of tears take me back somewhere or to somewhere?

Where I have come from doesn't exist, where I am

going I do not know. My sister says I need to learn to tread water.

So I try to teach myself to tread water in a pool of tears.

Love,
Gem

———

Dear Mum,
I want the shortcuts. I want to jump to the end.

This is not where the work is done. This is not how the work is done.

Love,
Gem

———

Dear Mum,
I was so angry. At you, at my husband, at the year of cancer. So angry I ripped everything down. So angry I found darkness and hid in it, pretending it might be light.

And now everything is still.

The world is still. The air is still. I am still.

Finally, I have nothing but grief three times distilled.

Every so often I reach out a hand. I ask, 'Will you be my friend?'

Love,
Gem

———

Dear Mum,

I visit your house sometimes, when my father isn't there. When he doesn't know.

I'm looking for you, for my family. Looking for the things that used to live there – love, laughter, a beating heart. Yes, arguments and tension and struggles as well.

It has gone quiet. Or, more precisely, it has gone cold.

The beautiful garden you worked on every day is nothing but plants gone to seed and gaps of dry earth. The fishpond you and my sister nourished is empty.

I remember the day I stupidly asked, 'Where did all these tiny fish come from?' and you replied, 'Do you really want me to answer that?'

We used to wonder how those fish would manage their booming population with us so reluctant to intervene. Why couldn't the magpies and kookaburras poach a few for us?

In the end, it took a broken heart for a caretaker. They vanished. Just like the warmth, the love, the laughter, the struggle.

Love,

Gem

Dear Mum,

I know I'm meant to carry parts of you with me. To keep you alive. For me . . . for others.

I just can't decide which parts.
Love,
Gem

———

Dear Mum,

I have your eyes. I have my father's mouth. I have a nose I made all on my own.

On my face, we are all together.

Some days I like this, others I want to be wholly me.

Love,
Gem

———

Dear Mum,

If my new partner walked into the room and you were there the two of you would talk for hours. You'd talk about books and films. You'd talk about art. You'd talk for the sake of talk.

If you watched my new partner working with your husband in the garden, you would smile knowingly – seeing something fall into place that had always been missing from our family.

If you could sneak a peek at the two of us alone, writing, reading, cooking, talking – all in the house you were so excited about – you would say, 'I watch the way the two of you work in synchrony; you work together.'

If you could see all of this, you would tell me, 'He is just right,' as though you were Goldilocks.
Love,
Gem

———

Dear Mum,
My sister is home. Your husband left town two days after she arrived.

Your daughters clean your kitchen together.

Your daughters weed your garden.

Together, we make your home home again.

Love,
Gem

———

Dear Mum,
Your husband... what can I even say about your husband?

Was he always like this? A child who needs scolding, who needs a parent? Or is this what happens when half of you unexpectedly vanishes?

Neither is an adequate explanation. Neither is an adequate excuse. For callousness, malice. For young women and cruel jokes. For absence.

I am worn out, worn down and worn through with your husband.

Love,
Gem

Dear Mum,

You used to talk about pain as music. Each type, a different note. You had so much of it, it must have sounded like a whole orchestra living in your body.

Sad times are high notes – piercing, screaming, desperate.

Good times are a low hum – playing along underneath conversations, drifting in and out.

Your absence fills my ears.

Love,

Gem

Dear Mum,

I was looking for some old blood test results of mine, and instead I found yours. The last ones I held in my hand, analysed, and recited to your husband.

I cried as though I was holding you.

Love,

Gem

CHAPTER TWENTY

I never knew grief could feel so much like fear

What about my grief? you might ask. How does grief manifest in the midst of these complex, fraught relationships? In the face of so much chaos?

Eight random facts:

1. Grief is different for every person.
2. Grief can manifest as panic.
3. The only place to get treatment for grief-induced panic attacks in the city where I live is in the same building that my mother died in.
4. We still don't know why some types of anti-anxiety medications can work for grief, given it is a natural process.

5. If you're really unlucky, some anti-anxiety medications can make your body flood your brain with adrenaline instead of serotonin.
6. A panic attack drenched in adrenaline should be called a terror attack.
7. Grief can make us feel as though we have no future.
8. Forty-five kilograms is not a healthy weight for an adult.

The knowledge my father gave me of my mother altered my grief. I was sad when she died, but I was also relieved – the suffering, the cancer, was over. And through it I had been transformed. I had faced things I'd never truly put to rest. Things that had drifted in and out of my thoughts chaotically for twenty years. More than anything, I had learnt that I mattered.

Knowing more fully what had happened to my mother took my grief beyond that initial relief, beyond simple sadness and loss. It made it deeper. It made it darker. Though that knowledge was itself so intertwined with more betrayal it's impossible to untangle which I was responding to.

In the weeks after the affair and finding out my mother's secrets, the only way I can describe my grief is smashing. That is to say, I smashed through grief.

First, I smashed my marriage. I gave up on the facade of our relationship. And so I broke the hands that had held me for nearly a decade, because they hadn't held me the way I needed. Especially during the year of cancer. Because I had changed so irrevocably that they could never hold me in the right way again.

Next, I smashed friendships. Some accidentally. Some deliberately, angry at people for failing to understand my grief.

While I slipped through the fingers and hands of those who did try to catch me, taking a hammer to some of them made me feel in control of my own freefall. It's the pieces I didn't break that hurt me – that took away my sense of control. The smashing of pieces by others turned my freefall into a plummeting drop to darkness.

Even when I wanted to grab, not smash, the hands that reached out to me, it was as if they had become coated in oil. So slippery they couldn't maintain their grasp on me, nor I on them. And as I slipped from the hands, rocks appeared – ripping off pieces of skin. Pieces of me.

As Nick Flynn wrote in his memoir *Another Bullshit Night in Suck City*, 'There are many ways to drown, only the most obvious wave their arms as they're going under.' Just like my father, I was going under.

———

After finding out about my father's mistress, for the first time in my life I began to suffer from panic attacks. They started small. Just a nervousness, a slight unease. Strangely, they occurred every day at 5 pm.

With each week, they would grow. Sitting at the hairdresser's one afternoon, flicking through my phone while I waited for my hair to turn the right shade of brown, it struck me: 'I'm not safe. I'm never going to be safe again.' Safe from what exactly wasn't clear; I just knew nothing was ever going to be okay again.

I never did work out what was so special about 5 pm, but like clockwork the attacks came, and by 7 pm they left. For months.

As the year wound on, they became less contained. They became relentless.

I stopped sleeping. I began running three times a day to try to keep them at bay. Through worry and exercise, I began to fade away.

I began to disappear; losing my matter all over again.

———

Dear Mum,

I'm right across the road from where I last saw you. I'm right across the road from where you died. In my own hospital bed. Exhaustion, anxiety, weight loss . . . it all added up. The irony – this is where I ended up, across the road from where we were last together.

Submitting to everything I've been trying to put a brave face on is a relief. But it's also sad. I know how

I never knew grief could feel so much like fear

I got here, I don't know how I got here. Either way, here I am.

It's like watching some other version of myself. There's me being checked into a hospital. There is me admitting she isn't coping anymore. There is me saying 'yes!' to medication after toughing it out for so long. There is a 'me' I no longer recognise. All I can hope is that there is another me I don't recognise, somewhere in the future, who doesn't look like this or feel like this.

In the meantime, the words of C.S. Lewis go round and round in my head: 'I never knew grief could feel so much like fear.'

Love,

Gem

Over the course of 2017 panic took over my body, finally landing me in hospital in October. I had always felt alone in 'family', but for the first ever I *was* truly alone. My mother was dead, my husband of ten years was gone and so were some of my closest friends. My father had become largely estranged from me – or, at best, strange to me – while my sister returned to the opposite side of the world and sparse communication.

For a while, I walked around the wide-open spaces of the house I'd built, with its high ceilings and giant glass windows capturing the sun. I would run my hands over the wooden kitchen bench, the back of the perfect blue sofa I had purchased, and wonder what my new life would look like and how I would find it. The house was beautiful, but for a time it also felt like more of a museum than a home. Perfectly in order. I had a three-bedroom house all to myself, but I slept, ate and watched movies on my laptop all in one room. My bedroom.

For the first six months, I never even turned on the stove, despite being a keen cook. The table I'd brought with me from Melbourne that seats ten, once used for raucous dinner parties, sat empty night after night.

I was waiting for my life to start again.

―

I lost friends. But more profoundly, I lost my father. Yes, he chose us over his mistress, but he never returned to us.

This realisation was most acute when sitting in a clinician's room, adjacent to a hospital bed I had been staying in for five days while doctors tried to stabilise my panic and weight loss.

While I was in hospital my father left for Sydney. He ran away again. When he returned, I demanded he come to my discharge meeting. You could call me an eternal optimist. You could also call me an eternal fool. Maybe these are the same thing?

Once again, I treated this as an attempt to reach through his grief to the person I used to know, to pull him back to us.

I wanted him in a room with doctors and psychologists to normalise the help-seeking. To destigmatise this type of care. It does not make you weak. In fact, it is what makes you stronger.

I wanted for him to hear about traumatic grief from an expert. I actually believed at the time that I too was suffering from traumatic grief, but the doctors insisted I wasn't. I was simplify worn down by my life, they told me. A rather ordinary diagnosis, I thought, for what felt like the end of the world.

'I know you said I don't have it, but can you describe the symptoms of traumatic grief?'

The doctor listed them: 'Irrational behaviour, outbursts of anger, avoidance, inappropriate emotional responses.'

I turned to my father. 'Do you think you have experienced any of these?'

'No,' he replied. Looking uncomfortably at his feet, a part of his body that you might reasonably think were a new species previously unknown to man, given his detailed study of them over the course of that year.

I try again. 'What do I need to be aware of, what should I look out for, the warning signs I might be moving into traumatic grief?'

The same list is repeated.

I turn to my father. 'If I develop these signs, can you tell me? Will you spot them? Will you let me or others know?'

'No,' he says. 'I cannot help you with your grief. I cannot

see these changes in you. You will have to rely on your friends to help you.'

The clinician shoots me a look. She sees the hurt in my eyes. We have prepared for this meeting. She knows I am trying to get help for him far more than I am trying to help myself, irrespective of how desperate my situation has become. I think she pitied me in that moment. But she could not help; she was experienced enough to know you can't save someone else from traumatic grief if they do not wish to be saved.

My father and I leave together in silence. We do not speak on the way back to my house. When he drops me off he says, 'I am too worn out from caring for your mother to help you now.'

I won't lie: it destroyed me when he said that. I've never felt more alone in all my life. More abandoned in all my life.

After everything I had given emotionally, he could give nothing in return.

During this time, I was so alone and fearful, but I wasn't *lonely*. I was exactly where I needed to be, as scary as it was to stand in that house and feel that in the space of eighteen months every part of my life that had felt dependable had been dismantled.

Every night that I crawled into bed in my empty house, every morning that I woke up with no one next to me,

I felt relief. People became too hard, for a time. They wanted more of me than I could give – they wanted to be heard, they wanted help, they wanted to connect. I had nothing left to offer anyone. I was done. And some of them were done with me.

There are lessons here about how I regained my footing. Some were about reaching for help. Some were about understanding the nature of grief.

Each day I kept my grief in, it made me small.

Each day I let it out, I grew and lost at the same time.

People will walk away from you because of grief. You don't realise that this is part of grieving until it happens, but it does – to almost everyone.

'I can't cope with all the drama in your life,' one friend texted me, and never wrote again. No one tells you in advance that when one thing crumbles, more will follow. And they don't tell you how that will make you feel.

Grief can make you feel as though there's nothing solid left in the whole world for you to stand on. As though every piece of the scaffolding of your life has been removed, and when you try to replace it with other things it's just a game of make-believe, an act of 'making do'. The new pieces, the struts you try to fix into place to hold yourself up, feel flimsy. You know in your heart they won't last. That new friend, that person you thought about dating; it's all just a stand-in for your actual life. A life that is somewhere behind you and will start again in earnest sometime in the future. But it isn't now, and you don't know how long 'now' will last for.

After a little while, you remove those flimsy stand-in struts, realising they were silly and didn't really belong. And on and on it goes, a process of trial and error. Until, little bit by little bit, things start to feel more solid again.

Little by little, I left my bedroom.

I hung painting on the walls, putting my mother's favourite piece of art in the living room.

I bought colourful rugs and placed them over the grey polished concrete floors.

When people were too much, I filled each room with plants.

Little by little, I brought the life back in.

In time, the stand-in struts were replaced by new foundations and proper scaffolding. Friends, old and new, who stood by me through it all – one of whom eventually became my new partner. And with him, a puppy and a cat joined the slow-moving couch that is my mountain dog, turning the house into a menagerie. In the evenings, we take walks around our garden, always with a gin in hand, and inspect the plants, attending to the individual needs of each. A little water, a particular fertiliser. We are making sure the life stays. That it grows.

We began trying to have a baby.

I never knew grief could feel so much like fear

In what was both a moment and an age, life started again.

I took the fancy job, the one my father doubted I could get; I became one of the youngest female associate professors in the country. This life I have built brings me joy – joy which has nothing to do with David or a desire to prove something, anything, to him. Or, for that fact, my mother.

I also became a writer of a different kind, beyond an academic. One who takes her darkest moments and lays them bare. Shares them around on a platter piled high with uncompromising truths spun through with metaphors and flickers of hope. Because there is nothing to be ashamed of in grief or suffering. If we live long enough, we all get lost, and we all lose things. One day, you will all join me on my island, through your own particular sorrows. In the end, despair unites us all.

One night I stood in a room of 150 strangers and read letters to my dead mother. I've spoken to audiences of 800 people, but nothing terrified me like that night. And I've never felt so whole.

None of these things would have been possible if my mother were still alive. I will never truly know what I lost and what I gained through her death; what I have done because she died, what I would have done if she had lived. Sometimes people say they'd 'give it all back', whatever 'it all' might be, to have someone they love not die. I don't know if that is true for me. My mother, in the fullness I now know, is my bones.

She holds me upright as I move through the day. But the life I have now, I'm not sure I would trade it in, for her or anything else I have lost, if someone offered it back to me.

When I stand in my living room, in the home I designed and built from the dirt up, I am no longer standing in a museum. Nothing is just for show; there is no facade. And you can open any drawer, lift any lid, without fear of finding secrets or chaos. Everything is exactly as it appears to be – for better or worse.

A hard-won honesty lives here.

———

Later, when I re-entered the world more fully, some people – family friends, people interstate – asked me why I had never reached out to them. Why I had never called. It is difficult for those removed from situations of intense grief to realise that simple acts like picking up the phone can become impossible. Instead we hunker down, wishing someone would notice and reach out to us, but also sometimes hoping that they won't.

As with most trauma, ultimately we must reach inwards. Realise what is truly happening and try to understand it. *Then* ask for help.

And so I did.

An email to my father, two weeks after my hospital discharge:

I know this will probably fall on deaf ears, but . . .

You carried a lot of caring of Mum through her chemotherapy. But I took a shitload of hits for the family last year. And they have left their mark on me.

I don't understand how you can just relinquish your role as parent because it's convenient for you right now.

We felt like a team when Mum had cancer.

I don't know what it's like to lose a partner of forty years, but I guess you can get a new partner. You can't get a new mum.

It would break her heart to see you abandoning me in the ways that you are.

Come back.

I never expected my email to have an effect. I'd long given up hope that my attempts to bring my father back to us, to me, would work. But I'm stubborn. And sometimes I need to say things just so I don't have to carry them around anymore. And so I sent it.

He never wrote back.

But soon after he began appearing at my house to work on the garden. With time, he came inside. He made conversation. Never about anything. Conversation for the sake of conversation. Because he did indeed care about what was happening to me.

He isn't the man he was. Our relationship is not what it was, nor what I hoped for. But it is the beginning of something new. And even if it isn't, my life has begun again. Only he can choose if he wants to be a part of it.

The year after my mother's cancer almost broke me. The people who walked away from me. The transformation of my father from parent to child to stranger.

But it didn't break me.

Among the many things I learnt was that relationships don't end when people die. They continue to evolve with you. And that can be the thing that saves you.

CHAPTER TWENTY-ONE

Something so hard should not be soft to the touch

If you've never scattered someone's ashes before you might think they're just that – ashes. Like the fine powdery residue you find at the bottom of the fireplace that's almost silky to the touch.

Human ashes aren't powdery. The remains of a cremated human body are more like gravel. Fine ash mixed with small stony pieces of bone. And so those gritty remains should be – something so hard should not be soft to the touch.

My mother's ashes sat in my father's walk-in wardrobe all year, sealed in an unceremonious grey plastic tub. She would have been so furious to know she'd been stuffed into a bottom drawer in the corner of my father's house.

I wanted my mother in the ocean. A woman who spent most of her life in chronic pain, she would say she felt weightless and free in the ocean. I wanted to take her back to the beach house, where she had spent her last weeks. She said in those weeks that she wished she'd been born a fish.

One rainy afternoon at the beach house, just before Christmas – ten months after my mother's death – I said to my sister, 'It's time.'

My sister and I walked down to the beach, a grey sky above us, storm rolling in, carrying that grey plastic tub with our mother's ashes inside. Our father stayed behind, unable to face the task at hand.

We waded into the surf, my sister bringing a Stanley knife. Once we were waist deep in the cold water, she cut a small hole in the top of the tub and handed it to me, not wanting to touch or look at the ashes.

I scattered the ashes all around me in circles. So much gravel poured through the small hole in the top of the tub. Slowly, I spun tiny fragments of bone, and they sank to the bottom of the ocean, bright white against the yellow sand, before being pulled out to sea by the next wave. On and on it went, layer after layer of bone, then sand, then bone again.

Sitting on the shore afterwards I felt heavy. It felt both deeply right and deeply wrong. My mother was where she belonged and yet I no longer had her. In a plastic tub at the bottom of a drawer wasn't exactly where I wanted to find my mother when I needed her, but at least it felt tangible.

Something so hard should not be soft to the touch

Now I had nothing. Yes, she was free – but she was also free from me.

Selfishly, I regretted what we'd just done. I wanted to run back into the ocean and find all those pieces of white bone. Scoop up the pieces in my hands and take them safely back home so I could still have my mother. Difficult, broken – traumatised – mother that she was, I understood her now in death better than I ever could have in life.

But my mother was gone. I could never speak to her about what I now knew. About abuse and trauma, about how difficult her husband could be. How I wanted to say that even though she hurt me so deeply, I understood. I didn't forgive her, but I did find new empathy for her. 'Sometimes,' as Rebecca Solnit writes, 'gaining and losing are more intimately related than we like to think.' I lost a whole life – a husband, a mother, a father. But I had gained a new one, built with tenacity from the ruins of the old. And I had built a new relationship with my mother, after her death.

With her ashes scattered, the knowledge that my life had changed irrevocably washed over me again. I had put myself back together, but her death – and the secrets we uncovered in the aftermath – have changed me. I will probably have to wait until the end of my life to truly understand the whole effect of these events.

My sister and I walked slowly back to the house as the rain began to fall, warm after the cold of the ocean.

One week later, my sister and I went back to the beach house. On a warm night we walked into the calm, dark ocean. As we stepped into the water, much warmer now, my sister shouted, 'Look!' Small sparkles moved about in the water around us. It was plankton: tiny, phosphorescent sea creatures drifting along the edge of an inky ocean.

I ran my hands through the water, watching the sparkles shoot off the tip of each finger. I waded further out and the green lights became brighter. Searching, I swam a hundred metres out to sea in the pitch-black night.

I spun in circles, much faster than on the day I scattered the bones. Now, instead of white fragments, a swirl of light surrounded me. Not bone on sand, but green on black. I spread my fingers and ran them through the water, each one creating its own little trail of sparks. I kicked my feet and a green glow spread out underneath me.

Looking up, the clear sky was full of stars – mirroring the sparkling lights I was creating in the ocean around me. It was as though in that vast ocean each of those white pieces of bone had come and found me again.

In that moment, I realised I knew exactly where to find my mother, and I always would.

My father, I am still searching for.

Something so hard should not be soft to the touch

Maybe I will always be searching for some kind of family.

Maybe I'll find it in myself.

Acknowledgements

This is a book I never imagined would get written. It is certainly not one that would have been published without the love and encouragement of a special few in my life: Ben O'Mara, David Sornig, Anna Spargo-Ryan and Lauren Deville.

A special thank you to my agent Sarah McKenzie for believing my book had a message the world needed to hear, and Jane Palfreyman for agreeing with her. Finally, Ali Lavau for understanding that organising the words on the page in the way you want is just as important as the story itself.

Grateful acknowledgement is made to the following for permission to reprint extracts from previously published material

David Harrower, *Blackbird*, 2005, reprinted with permission of Faber and Faber, London

C.S. Lewis, *A Grief Observed*, 1961, reprinted with permission of Faber and Faber Ltd, London

Audre Lorde, 'The Transformation of Silence into Language and Action', *Sister Outsider*: *Essays and speeches*, 1984, originally published by Crossings Press

Maggie O'Farrell, *I Am, I Am, I Am: Seventeen brushes with death*, 2017, reprinted with permission of Headline Publishing, London

Josephine Wilson, *Extinctions,* 2017, reprinted with permission of UWA Publishing, Crawley, Western Australia